I loved this book! I on the road to God. It ta how God protected her t.. w..... way. She says you're a queen in training. We need to have patience and love for God. This book put my eyes on God and not on my surroundings. This book is good for adults too because it tells how you can take care of your teen.

- Sophie, 11

I love the book! It's really good for teens and adults. It is about Esther and how she saved her people, the Jews, from annihilation. This book really points away from all of that and into the greatness of our God. I would recommend this to my friends.

- Bianca, 13

This was a wonderful exercise for the girls. I am always on the look-out for devotions geared towards the girl's age group. I am trying to help them gain a hunger for His word! This book is a great way to teach them how to better understand the layers entwined in God's Word. It provides timeless applications and shows how we, like Esther, may not see or hear God in a season of life but He certainly is always present. It was a nice surprise to see my girls reading the books on their own and the smiles from their many AHA moments!

- Sandy, mother of two

This study of Queen Esther was good. I found it in-depth and comparable to many of the Bible studies I've done. At the same time doing a great job of explaining terms and concepts that many teens and new Christians may not be familiar with. I found myself learning things that have surprised me, not having seen them in 35 years of active church life!

- Aryn, blogger, and founder of Aryn the Libraryan

Royal:

Life Lessons
from the
Book of Esther

Also by Aminata Coote

How To Find Your Gratitude Attitude
Face Your Fears: Choose Faith Over Fear
7 Lessons on Endurance from Hebrews 12:1-2
Through God's Eyes: Marriage Lessons for Women

Royal:

Life Lessons
from the
Book of Esther

Aminata Coote

GIRLS OF
1
EXCELLENCE

Names: Coote, Aminata (Christian blogger) author

Title: Royal: Life Lessons from the Book of Esther / Aminata Coote
Identifiers: ASIN: B07VKG4YRM | ISBN: 9781072256465
Subjects: Young Adult Nonfiction—Religion—Biblical Stories & Studies | Social Topics—Values & Virtues

Cover design by Marco Coote and Aminata Coote

Images courtesy of Canva.com

Dedication

To the girl who needs to learn she is valuable beyond compare.

Contents

Introduction

I am writing this book for the girl who struggles to be kind to herself and to other girls. I get it. I truly do. Life is hard and it seems as though all those other girls try to take for themselves resources and things you feel rightly belong to you. You feel as though you must fight to defend your little space of the world. Or, lose it forever and then no one will ever know who you were.

I'm writing this book for the girl who struggles to be herself. For years you've been told to be like some other person. You've been told to sit and be quiet or to get up and be more active. It seems as though everyone wants you to be someone other than who you are.

I'm writing to the girl who struggles to love herself. After hearing for the umpteenth time that you're not like So-and-So, you start to believe something must be wrong with being you. So you scratch and bite as you try to be like those other persons while thinking you must be unlovable and that's why no one wants you to be you.

I'm writing to introduce you to the One who created you before your parents even thought about having children. The One who has a plan for your life and is willing to use even the bad things for His glory. Because before you can change the world, you need to know what is expected of you. You have to hone the skills God has given you.

That's what this book is about. On the surface, it's a Bible study of the book of Esther but it's so much more. It's about leadership and learning to be kind. It's about learning to love yourself so you can step into your true identity. It's about treating each other with respect. Because if we can't do those things, we'll be trapped in our mean girl personas forever. But if we can master those few skills (and others not covered in this book), we can inhabit the space God has created for us.

Before we dig into the lessons found in the book of Esther, let's talk about what life skills are and why they matter.

For us to survive in this world, we have to be able to do a number of things. So things like feeding yourself, bathing or tying your shoelaces are examples of life skills. As are numeracy and literacy skills. There will be things that I need to know that you won't and vice versa. The skills we need depend on where we live, age, our life circumstance, and even our culture. Basically, a life skill is an ability that helps us to deal effectively with the challenges of being alive. And sometimes, life can be a real challenge.

Don't worry; we're not going to talk about hygiene or the right way to tie your shoelaces. Instead, we're going to focus on things like character, honor and walking with God.

As we go through this book I'm going to ask a few things of you:

1. Read the book of Esther—it's a short Bible book (only ten chapters and it's an engaging story). This will give you the context of the story that I'll reference throughout this book. If you choose to listen instead of reading, it will take you less than an hour to listen to the entire book. I have created a playlist on YouTube which has multiple translations. Choose the one you like best. You can access those videos through this URL: https://bit.ly/2GOEQR4.

From time to time, I will mention a particular chapter or include passages from Esther which I want us to focus on. I'll do my best to give you some of the history surrounding the events so that it makes sense to you.

2. Think about what you're reading—I mean really think about it. Imagine yourself in the situations presented and answer the questions that are included. Be honest with yourself. Don't think about who may read your thoughts or anything. It's just you, me and God. I promise not to say anything and I know He won't either.

3. Journal your thoughts—there are a number of questions throughout this book. You'll get a better experience if you

actually pause to think about them and write your answers down. If you choose to write them down, your answers will serve as material you can revisit later to remember the lessons you learned. This is not going to be like homework. There are no wrong or right answers. No one is going to check what you wrote or grade you for handwriting or grammar, so be as honest as you'd like in your responses.

4. Most of all, have fun! Yes, reading the Bible and learning more about God can, and should, be interesting. Try to imagine yourself in the palace and then try to figure out how the lessons apply to you. If you get stuck on anything or want to ask a question, email me at Aminata@hebrews12endurance.com, I'll respond as soon as I can.

Now that you know what to expect, let's get started!

Your Bible study partner,

Aminata

A Queen...

Don't let anyone look down on you because you are young, but set an example for the believers in speech, in conduct, in love, in faith and in purity.

— 1 Timothy 4:12 NIV

1

What a Queen Is Not

*B*efore we start talking about all the skills we're going to learn to rule the world, let's talk a little about what not to do. Much of this will be in the context of the Bible book we're exploring, but I know you'll find ways to connect it to your life. I'm sure of it.

You will need your Bible because we're going to spend a lot of time in Esther. If you're having a hard time finding the book of Esther, it's nestled between Nehemiah and Job. There's something significant about the placement of Esther's story. Her story is snuggled between the tales of a man who was instrumental in rebuilding Jerusalem's wall while she was queen, and one who walked faithfully with God centuries before she had been born.

Our story begins in a palace. During the third year of his reign, King Xerxes[1] held a banquet for all his nobles and officials. This banquet lasted six months. Now before you start thinking every official was away from their post for an extended period of time, that's probably not what happened. Historians and Bible scholars believe the officials went to Xerxes on a schedule[2]. Maybe he sent missives and told them when to appear. Or, he had them choose the time they wanted to attend the banquet. Based on what history says about Xerxes, it's more likely he told them when to appear and they showed up.

At the end of the six-month banquet, Xerxes had a week-long feast which was open to everyone who lived in the land—even the commoners. This party was unusual for its time. Usually, at a banquet such as this, the host would set limits on how much people could drink[3]. If the limit was three glasses, everyone had to drink three glasses whether you wanted to or not. But in this case, there were no rules. The king opened his wine cellar and everyone could drink as much—or as little—as he wanted.

On the final day of the feast, he sent his seven chamberlains[4] (think attendants) to ask his wife—Queen Vashti—to appear before him and the men gathered in the banquet hall. She refused. The king became angry and asked his advisors what should be done to punish her. Their suggestion was he should depose[5] her from her position. She would be banished from his presence and would no longer be the queen.

You may think that's a harsh punishment for not doing something foolish. Maybe you're a little mad because feminine pride made you side automatically with Quee.. Vashti. So let's look at the background.

In 485 BC, Xerxes became king of a vast empire which stretched from India to Ethiopia—a distance of 4,317 kilometers[6]—and was divided into 127 provinces. A province simply referred to the division of a country. If this was a modern community they would probably say town or city.

Persia-Media was the dominant world power at that time. They had defeated a great number of nations and had captured many people. To keep the peace, they set governors or satraps over each province and sub-division. Xerxes was on the brink of war with Greece. Ten years earlier, his father King Darius, had tried to conquer the Greeks but hadn't been able to do so before his death[7]. Darius had suffered a humiliating defeat. Xerxes wanted to redeem his father in the eyes of the people (and conquer some new territory while he was at it).

Xerxes banquet

This banquet was a show of power. He wanted to garner the support of his people—financially, politically and nominally. It would also prove to the men who would lead his troops and fight in his army that he had more than enough money to fund the campaign. At the same time, each man would pledge a certain sum to support the campaign. But the banquet wasn't all fun and games. It would have been a time for the commanders of the army to meet and discuss ideas for the battles ahead. It was a strategic meeting.

While Xerxes met with the men, Queen Vashti presided over a banquet for the women. She played her role to gain the support of the wives. As the king filled the men's heads with visions of victory in battle, Vashti would have painted for their women a picture of the beauty and splendor of the kingdom. These women would be left all alone for the duration of the war. They needed to find their own reasons to support it. They would need a reason to get them through the lonely nights ahead—especially if their men did not come home.

The men of Susa had spent the last seven days—some of them more—drinking. The Bible tells us that on the seventh day of the feast, the king was merry with wine (Esther 1:10 ESV). I'm guessing King Xerxes was a happy drunk. I imagine him telling jokes and tall tales which became more expansive as he drank. The courtyard sparkled with lights and the men got louder and rowdier as the night went on. The men who couldn't hold their liquor had fallen into a drunken stupor but that did not discourage the others from drinking.

Then the king had the best idea: he had shown the men all that he owned—his beautiful palace, the personalized gold goblets, the gold, and silver lounging couches, and beautiful tapestries in the nation's colors—why not show them his most prized possession? Why not show them his queen? Before you start grumbling that Vashti was not something to be owned, let's remember the context—that's just how it was in those days. A man may love his wife but in the eyes of the law, she was considered his property in the same way he owned an animal or a piece of land.

Xerxes sent his seven attendants to summon his queen so she could appear before the men. But she refused:

On the seventh day, when King Xerxes was in high spirits from wine, he commanded the seven eunuchs who served him—Mehuman, Biztha, Harbona, Bigtha, Abagtha, Zethar and Karkas—to bring before him Queen Vashti, wearing her royal crown, in order to display her beauty to the people and nobles, for she was lovely to look at. But when the attendants delivered the king's command, Queen Vashti refused to come. Then the king became furious and burned with anger (Esther 1:10–12 NIV).

You may wonder what was wrong with Vashti's reaction. After all, it was perfectly reasonable to refuse a request that could have been humiliating for her. Well, it was and it wasn't. When we read accounts in the Bible we tend to read them with a modern, Western-flavored mindset. Remember what I said about women being considered the man's property?

Well, Persian kings considered themselves as gods[8]. And even if they hadn't, he was her ruler. I mean, if the prime minister or president of your country gave you a direct command you wouldn't refuse, would you? I bet even if your principal or pastor instructed you to do something you'd do it. Maybe you wouldn't like it very much, but you'd comply.

When Vashti refused to obey her husband, the king— and as far as the Persian-Medes were concerned, their god—it shifted the balance of power. They were about to invade a country and conquer its people. If the king couldn't command his own wife, how would he be able to command a whole army of men? What would happen when their wives heard that the queen disobeyed a direct order from the king? And let's not forget: many of these women would have witnessed Vashti's refusal firsthand.

There are many theories about why Vashti refused. Some say she refused because the king wanted her to appear wearing only her crown[9]. Others say it was because it was forbidden for Persian women, especially the queen, to be exposed to public view[10]. Some believe she was pregnant with her son Artaxerxes at the time[11]. But here's what I want us to focus on: her reason doesn't matter.

It was about obedience. One of the biggest lessons we'll have to learn in our life is how to obey. We must obey our parents and those set above us (authority figures like teachers, police officers, and people at church). But above all, we have to learn to obey God.

> *One of the biggest lessons we'll have to learn in our life is how to obey.*

Vashti disobeyed her husband and king. While she may have had valid reasons, her actions had potentially far-reaching effects. What had the wives thought when the queen refused to go to her husband when he called? If the queen didn't obey her husband, was it okay for them to disobey their husbands? Were they also allowed to disobey the king?

Meanwhile, the men waited for the queen to appear but she didn't. Drunk though they were, some of them may have considered it a sign of disrespect, not only for her husband—the king—but also of themselves. There are those who think Memucan[12] exaggerated the situation for his own benefits—and maybe he did—but surely some of the men wondered at the implications for their own wives. If the queen did not submit to her husband, why should the other women?

Leaders lead

You see, queen Vashti had the eyes of the entire kingdom on her but she didn't think about how her actions would make the king appear in front of his men. She didn't think of the impact her refusal would have on the women over whom she presided. In a similar way, people are observing the way you behave and some may be imitating your behavior.

As a leader, it's important to think about the people you lead. Now you may be thinking, "I'm not a leader." Yes, my dear friend, you are. God called His people to be a nation of priests and kings (1 Peter 2:9). This identity was first given to the nation God called to serve Him[13]—the Israelites—and it applies to us. This identity will follow us all the way to heaven. The Bible teaches that those who die in Christ will be "the priests of God and of Christ and will reign with [God] one thousand years" (Revelation 20:6)[14].

We need to understand that people will note our actions and mimic them—even if we would rather they didn't. When you imagine a queen, what do you think about? (You can write your answer on page 22.)

If you've watched any movies about royalty, you're probably thinking a queen should be demure, soft-spoken and ladylike. And you'd be right (to a point). Queens and princesses behave in ways which represent their countries at all times—even when they're having fun or at school. They need to be able to quickly analyze a situation and figure out

How should a queen behave?

....

....

....

....

....

....

....

....

....

the most appropriate thing to do or the best way to act. And then, they have to take their own advice. Being a leader is a bit like being a queen-in-training. You have to know how to react in every situation. There are going to be times when your emotions tell you to react in a certain way, but your mind tells you to respond differently. You will have to learn to choose the reaction which best represents your kingdom and fits the situation.

Ambassadors for Christ

Before we go any further, let's talk about who we're representing. 2 Corinthians 5:20 tells us we are ambassadors for Christ, but what does it mean to be an ambassador?

An ambassador is someone who serves as a representative for another person, company or country. The ambassador behaves or speaks in a manner consistent with the values of the one who sent them. Many people will never see the person whom the ambassador represents. That's why it's good to make a positive impression.

Because we are ambassadors for Christ, we represent Him wherever we go. Whether or not people know we are Christians, we show them who Christ is through our actions and words.

An ambassador:

....

....

....

....

....

....

....

....

....

....

Since we are representing Christ, you may want to know a little about who He is so we need to do a bit of research. Get your Bible and let's do some exploration. Note what each verse tells you about Jesus.

- 1 John 5:20
- Matthew 16:15–16
- John 1:1-4
- Philippians 2:5–8
- Hebrews 4:14–15
- Revelation 1:5
- John 10:30
- 1 Timothy 2:5

From these verses, we learn some things about Jesus. He is:

- The Son of God (Matthew 16:15–16).
- Creator of all things (John 1:3).
- The servant of God (Philippians 2:5–8).
- Our high priest (Hebrews 4: 14–15).
- The faithful witness, firstborn of the dead, and the ruler of kings on earth (Revelation 1:5).
- United with God, the Father (John 10:30).
- The mediator between us and God, the Father (1 Timothy 2:5).

And we represent Him! That means we have to behave in ways which give glory to God and make others want to know more about Him. Are you being a good ambassador for the King of kings?

As queen, Vashti represented King Xerxes and the 127 provinces of Persia-Media. She represented the forthcoming campaign to Greece and all the hopes and dreams her husband had to conquer new lands. Was Vashti being a good ambassador?

How we respond to authority has a lot to do with our heart attitude. Our heart attitude has to do with our motivations and whether we're doing things for the right reasons. How do you respond to the authority figures in your life?

2

The Characteristics of a Queen

*T*he second chapter of Esther began with a repentant Xerxes. He was no longer angry and he didn't have a queen. Bible scholars believe there was a period of two years between the events of chapters one and two. During that time, Xerxes had been in Greece[1]. He had a harem full of women, but his official partner had been deposed and could no longer appear before him[2].

So, why he didn't just reverse his decision, allow Vashti to apologize and restore her as queen? Well you see, when a Persian king made an edict, declaration or law, it could not be reversed[3].

And even if he could reverse it, he wouldn't have wanted to because he had sent news across his entire kingdom that

Vashti was no longer queen. How do you think he would have looked in the eyes of his subjects? He wouldn't want them to have even a niggling impression that he was not completely in charge—especially after the defeat in Greece. His advisors were once again quick to offer him a solution.

Then the king's personal attendants proposed, "Let a search be made for beautiful young virgins for the king. Let the king appoint commissioners in every province of his realm to bring all these beautiful young women into the harem at the citadel of Susa. Let them be placed under the care of Hegai, the king's eunuch, who is in charge of the women; and let beauty treatments be given to them. Then let the young woman who pleases the king be queen instead of Vashti." This advice appealed to the king, and he followed it (Esther 2:2-4 NIV).

There are a lot of things happening in these verses, let me explain a few of them. Though the king had a number of concubines, we can assume none of them pleased him enough to be elevated to the status of queen wife[4]. And, as we have already seen, Xerxes had a taste for unique things.

Virgins are taken

His men would, therefore, bring all the beautiful, young virgins to the king. You may have already picked it up but let me explain further—these women would not be given a choice. This wasn't like a season of The Bachelor[5] where an invitation would be sent out and women would apply for the honor of being the next queen.

It was more like Taken. The men appointed would go house to house procuring women who were young, believed to be virgins, and who met the king's standard of beauty. These women would be taken to the palace and put under virtual house arrest in the harem. They would never leave the palace again. They would spend their first year in the harem being given beauty treatments.

Before each young woman was taken to the king's bed, she was given the prescribed twelve months of beauty treatments—six months with oil of myrrh, followed by six months with special perfumes and ointments (Esther 2:12 NLT).

The oil of myrrh was chosen because it made the skin soft and smooth. It also had a high fragrance to mask the smell of sweat and other odors because Persia was hot[6] and bathing rituals were not as they are now.

The twelve months ritual was a way of ensuring the king was not burdened by a child who was not his[7]. While the men chose women they thought were virgins, they would have been unable to examine them to confirm because to do so would violate a woman set aside for the king, possibly their future queen. Men had been executed for less!

One of the virgins was a young woman named Hadassah, well her pet name was Esther but for the rest of this book, she will only be called Esther. Some scholars believe she may have been given the name Esther by her cousin and foster father Mordecai to protect her Jewish heritage[8].

Others believe the king named her Esther after she became queen[9]. Hadassah is a Jewish name which means myrtle, while Esther is a Persian name which means star.

Esther may have been a reference to the Babylonian goddess Ishtar[10]. Babylon had become an important city in Persia after it had been captured by King Cyrus (Xerxes' grandfather) in 539 BC[11]. It was a common practice at the time to have one's name refer to a pagan god[12].

It's also interesting to note that the myrtle flower has five points and is similar in appearance to a star. The name Esther was a bit of both worlds and hints at the role she would play as the mediator between two cultures.

Who is a Jew?

So why was it important to note that Esther was a Jew? Who were the Jews? In Genesis 12:1, God called Abraham to leave his people and promised he would become the father of many nations. They would be given a great and prosperous land to settle in. About four hundred years later, Abraham's descendants inherited the land of Canaan. They called the land Israel after one of their ancestors[13]. The people we know as the Jews were also called Hebrews or Israelites.

The word Jew comes from the Hebrew word Yehudi which is derived from the name Judah, who was one of Jacob's (Abraham's descendant) twelve sons. Originally, the term Yehudi was used specifically for members of the tribe of Judah. However, after King Solomon's death, the nation of Israel was split into two kingdoms: Judah and Israel (1 Kings 12; 2 Chronicles 10). After that time, the word Yehudi was used to describe anyone from the kingdom of Judah, which included the tribes of Judah, Benjamin, and Levi, as well as scattered settlers from other tribes.

In the 6th century BC, Israel was conquered by Assyria and the ten tribes were exiled from the land (2 Kings 17). Only the kingdom of Judah remained in the land of Canaan. These people from the kingdom of Judah were generally known as Yehudim (Jews), and the name continues to be used today[14].

The Hebrews had been set apart as God's chosen people. They had received a set of guidelines on how to live and worship, including the Ten Commandments found in Exodus 20:1–17. Some of those guidelines made them appear peculiar. They were forbidden from eating certain meats such as camels, rabbits, pigs or snakes. You can read more about this in Leviticus 11. They dressed and groomed themselves differently and abided by certain purity laws such as the ceremonial washing of hands[15].

> *Any woman can become a queen as long as she meets certain requirements.*

In 597 BC, Jerusalem fell after a three-month-long siege by King Nebuchadnezzar of Babylon. The people of Jerusalem were taken captive. This happened after many years of idolatry which God had warned them to avoid. When Esther was taken to the palace, the Jews had been in Babylon 118 years[16]. During the reign of Cyrus the Great, they had been given permission to re-inhabit their land, but many of them remained in the Persia[17].

The young Jewess was taken to the palace where she would have to live with other women from pagan nations. She would be set apart. It's possible Mordecai asked her to keep her nationality a secret because he did not want her to be treated differently because of her religious beliefs. I believe it was Providence—God had a purpose and a plan for Esther so He put her in the palace under this unique set of circumstances.

There's a lesson here I don't want us to miss. Any woman could become queen as long as she met certain requirements:

- She was beautiful.
- She was young.
- She was a virgin.
- She pleased the king.

Let's look at each one in turn.

The Queen is Beautiful

Let's dig into the word beauty in the original Hebrew language. The word that we read as fair or beautiful in our English Bible is the Hebrew word towb (pronounced tobe).

Other ways to translate it are good, best, better, bountiful, cheerful, at ease, graciously, joyful, kindly, kindness, loving, merry, precious, sweet, or well-favoured[18].

I believe the original language speaks to the way God sees us. When He created the first people, they were perfect. It was disobedience which led to sin and separated us from God. Our Heavenly Father wants to restore His perfect imprint to us. This happens through the blood of His Son Jesus Christ. When we accept Jesus as our Lord and Savior, God takes away the ugly sin that we're wrapped in and clothes us in the beauty of Christ's righteousness (Isaiah 61:10, 64:6)[19]. Our perfect condition is restored in the sight of God because He no longer sees us when we come before Him, He sees His perfect Son.

It is important to note that God does not see beauty the way men do. For God, beauty has little to do with outward appearance and everything to do with our heart (1 Samuel 16:7).

What motivates you? What are the thoughts that you wouldn't want anyone to know? God knows everything about you and yet He loves you. He loves you with the kind of love that will pursue you wherever you go.

The Queen is Young

Solomon, the wisest man who ever lived, wrote:

"Remember also your Creator in the days of your youth, before the evil days come and the years draw near of which you will say, 'I have no pleasure in them;'" (Ecclesiastes 12:1 ESV).

The original Hebrew word translated young is na'ărâh (pronounced nah-ar-aw'). It means a girl (from infancy to adolescence), damsel, maiden, young woman[20].

God calls us when we are young and have the fervor and vigor to serve Him actively and with enthusiasm. God wants us to have the experience King David did:

> From birth I have relied on you;
> you brought me forth from my mother's womb.
> I will ever praise you.
> Since my youth, God, you have taught me,
> and to this day I declare your marvelous deeds.
> Even when I am old and gray,
> do not forsake me, my God,
> till I declare your power to the next generation,
> your mighty acts to all who are to come
> (Psalm 71:6, 17–18 NIV).

It's not that we can't serve Him when we're old, but God wants us to spend our lives developing our relationship with Him. The more time we spend getting to know God, the more we will learn to rely on Him.

The Queen is a Virgin

The original Hebrew word translated virgin is bᵉthûwlâh (pronounced beth-oo-law'). It means to separate; a virgin (from her privacy); sometimes (by continuation) a bride; maid, virgin[21]. Virginity in the Bible sometimes symbolizes purity. Jesus told His disciples the parable of the ten virgins. If you have never heard the parable, please read it in Matthew 25:1–13.

The ten virgins were going to a wedding. As they waited on the bridegroom, they fell asleep. They were woken by the cry: "The bridegroom's coming! The bridegroom's coming!" All ten awoke to find that their lamps had gone out, but only five of them had extra oil. These five women were able to go

> *Those who will reign with God after the Second Coming are those who remain pure while on earth.*

on to the wedding feast while the others had to try to find oil for their lamps. By the time they got to the celebration, it had been too late and they were denied entrance.

All of these women were pure, so why did some get to meet the bridegroom while some didn't? It's about preparation. Oil represents the Holy Spirit. Five of the virgins were sealed (kept pure) by the Holy Spirit, but five weren't. Purity is required to make it into the kingdom of God, but it's not a case of once pure always pure. Nor is it a case of once unclean, always unclean.

Or do you not know that wrongdoers will not inherit the kingdom of God? Do not be deceived: Neither the sexually immoral nor idolaters nor adulterers nor men who have sex with men nor thieves nor the greedy nor drunkards nor slanderers nor swindlers will inherit the kingdom of God. And that is what some of you were. But you were washed, you were sanctified, you were justified in the name of the Lord Jesus Christ and by the Spirit of our God (1 Corinthians 6 NIV).

Those who will reign with God after the Second Coming are those who remain pure while on earth. We are required to put away old behaviors and take on new ones if we expect to be queens in heaven with God.

The Queen Pleases the King

Anyone can reign with God as long as they meet His requirements:

- We accept Jesus as our Savior (Romans 10:9).
- We commit to serve Him (Colossians 3:23-25).
- We keep His commandments (John 14:15).
- We keep ourselves pure (Matthew 5:8).

Our loyalty must first and foremost be to God. As we seek to be ambassadors for the Great King, we must avoid certain things. That means sometimes we won't be able to do as we see our friends do or speak as they do.

When Jesus returns, we will be asked to account for every word we speak (Matthew 12:36). And, we will be judged for our actions—whether good or bad (2 Corinthians 5:10).

What motivates me?

....

....

....

....

....

....

....

....

....

3

Who Do You Want to Be?

Before we continue, you must decide if you want to be a queen. Esther was not given a choice, but you have one. Do you want to reign with Jesus for a thousand years? If you want to be a queen, tell Him now. Pray: "Jesus, I want to reign with You in heaven, please forgive me of my sins. I accept You as my Lord and Savior, in Your name I pray, amen."

Now you have to make the decision to move away from your past. Accept God's forgiveness and try to stop doing the things you did that you know are wrong. It won't be easy, but with the help of the Holy Spirit, it is possible.

From this moment, you're a queen-in-training. You're going to have to walk away from some of your friends and change some of your hobbies and habits.

You will also have to learn to do new things like reading—and studying—your Bible, praying and using your talents and gifts to serve God. Service looks different for each of us because we all have different skills and abilities. If you want to learn more about how you can start using your spirituals gifts, check out the blog post https://bit.ly/UsingGifts.

Learning to be more like Jesus is a process you will go through every day for the rest of your life. I don't say this to discourage you; I say it to remind you that even though you're

If you fall, confess your sin to Jesus and ask Him to forgive you.

striving for perfection, you're not perfect. We won't be perfect as long as we live on a sinful Earth so you have to learn to give yourself grace. If you fall, confess your sin to Jesus and ask Him to forgive you. The Bible tells us that if we confess our sins, God is faithful and just. He will forgive us our sins and purify us from all unrighteousness (1 John 1:9).

What things in my past will I need to put behind me?

What about our characters?

As we read the first chapter of Esther, we get glimpses of the man who ruled Persia-Media. While it's not good to make sweeping generalizations about people, we start to get an idea about who Xerxes was. The king was:

Flamboyant—anyone who held a feast for six months must have a bit of a showy personality.

Shrewd—the banquet was done strategically. This wasn't a random party so the king could have some fun; it was a systematic attempt to win the approval and financial support for a costly expedition.

Impulsive—the decision to ask Vashti to appear before him was done with little thought to the protocol or cultural norms.

Easily influenced—the punishment suggested by Memucan for Vashti's refusal seems a little extreme. Chances are it was approved because Memucan was one of the king's trusted advisors. Xerxes did not question what his advisor suggested, he just did it. As we read more of Esther, we see this trait repeated.

Selfish—Xerxes didn't think about how Vashti would have felt to be summoned away from her guests for the entertainment of his. He didn't think about how the women would have felt to be deprived of the queen's presence when they had been specifically invited to her ball.

Xerxes was a king, but he had some traits which are not admirable in a leader. Do you like working with someone who did whatever they pleased without consulting the rest of the group? Or, considering how it would affect everyone

A good leader...

else's grades? The phrase "if it pleases the king" is repeated throughout the book of Esther and tells us the kind of leader Xerxes was. He did what pleased him regardless of how it affected others.

I'd like you to spend some time thinking about the type of influence you want to leave. What do you want people to say about you? What do you want them to think about you? Please understand that we can't control what people say or think about us, but we can do our best to behave in a manner which represents our values and the God whom we serve.

Our attitude says a lot

Let's look at how Esther behaved after she was taken from her home and family. Even if she was not chosen to be queen, she would be one of the king's concubines and unable to leave the palace. She would never see her cousin Mordecai again. Did she have reasons to be unhappy? You bet. But look at her behavior when she got to the palace:

She pleased him [Hegai] and won his favor. Immediately he provided her with her beauty treatments and special food. He assigned to her seven female attendants selected from the king's palace and moved her and her attendants into the best place in the harem (Esther 2:9 NIV).

Does that sound like a young woman who was grumpy and solemn? Since we don't know how many women were taken to the palace in Susa, let's imagine one woman from each province—127 in all. In the midst of all those beautiful women, something about Esther pleased Hegai. I mean, come on, this man had been emasculated and dehumanized (the name Hegai simply means eunuch[1]); she had no reason to be kind to him.

Yet, she not only pleased him but won his favor. He was so charmed by her he expedited her beauty treatments. He also gave her the best accommodations available. I imagine having the favor of the eunuch in charge made her life more miserable. It may have gone a little bit like this:

The harem was filled with beautiful, young ladies from all over the kingdom. Within the first few days, lines were drawn. Some of them came from humble homes. They stared wide-eyed at the gold and silver couches and the purple, blue and white curtains. At mealtimes, they looked at the food presented as if they had never seen the likes of such before. They looked to the left and then to the right and began piling their plates with as much meat as it could hold.

Across the hall were the privileged ones. They came from wealthy families and had been given everything they desired for as long as they had been alive. They scorned the girls who came from poorer families as if poverty were somehow contagious. Though they ate together and gathered in a group to criticize the rest of the girls, they were not friends. They were competitors. Each girl thought they had the right to be queen and nothing was going to get in her way.

One girl walked alone. She didn't fit into any of the cliques. Oh, she was nice enough to everyone, but she didn't join the group who spent their time criticizing the other girls. She didn't appear to be overwhelmed by the luxury of the palace. She spoke softly to the chamberlains and maidens who were assigned to assist the girls. Most times she sat by the window looking out at the people who passed by. Every once in a while she smiled with delight but for the most part, she was quiet.

What kind of influence do I want to leave?

....

....

....

....

....

....

....

....

How many times have you seen beautiful people being unkind to those whom they consider inferior to themselves? I have seen it too many times—especially among young girls—and it's painful to watch. God tells us to bear each other's burdens (Galatians 6:2), but too many times we are more interested in tearing each other down instead of building each other up.

Esther wasn't like that. From her we learn three key lessons:

1. **We need to be obedient**—Esther was raised by her cousin Mordecai. We don't know how old either of them was, but since Mordecai adopted Esther as his daughter, we can assume there was a significant age difference (Esther 2:7). Esther respected Mordecai by being obedient and submissive to him. When she was taken into the palace, Mordecai told her not to reveal her nationality to anyone. She kept her secret until Mordecai told her to share it with the king (Esther 4:13–16).

Unfortunately, obedience is becoming a lost art. Our society teaches that we need to be independent thinkers and should not depend on anyone. Somehow this has translated into a lack of regard for others. Do you know someone who disobeys authority? Are there girls (and boys) at your church or school who try to defy the adults they come in contact with?

How about you? What's your attitude towards authority figures? Do you obey your parents, teachers and other adults set above you? Do you obey the persons elected to student government?

Obedience is a required skill for queens-in-training. Keeping God's commandments is one of the requirements to reign with Him in heaven. Here are some things the Bible says about obedience:

Remind them to be submissive to rulers and authorities, to be obedient, to be ready for every good work (Titus 3:1 ESV).

Slaves, obey in everything those who are your earthly masters, not by way of eye-service, as people-pleasers, but with sincerity of heart, fearing the Lord. Whatever you do, work heartily, as for the Lord and not for men, knowing that from the Lord you will receive the inheritance as your reward. You are serving the Lord Christ. For the wrongdoer will be paid back for the wrong he has done, and there is no partiality (Colossians 3:22-25 ESV).

Have confidence in your leaders and submit to their authority, because they keep watch over you as those who must give an account. Do this so that their work will be a joy, not a burden, for that would be of no benefit to you (Hebrews 13:17 NIV).

Everyone must submit to governing authorities. For all authority comes from God, and those in positions of authority have been placed there by God (Romans 13:1 NLT).

Each of these verses teaches that we need to obey those set above us. When we do, we please the Lord.

We sharpen our ability to obey God, as we learn to obey the individuals who are set above us. If we can't obey people we can see, we won't be able to obey God whom we cannot see.

How Obedient Are You?

1. When my mom tells me to put down the phone and do my homework, I...

a. Put down the phone immediately and do as she tells me.
b. Finish what I'm doing and then do my homework.
c. Do my homework while still using my phone.
d. Pretend I did not hear.
e. Lie and tell her I've already finished my homework

2. I really want to go to the mall with my friends but my parents say I can't go, do I...

a. Call my friends and tell them I can't go.
b. Tell my friends I can't go but make sure my parents know how unhappy I am about their decision.
c. Beg and plead until they agree.
d. Make plans to go the next day.
e. Go anyway but don't tell my parents.

3. I'm talking with my friends after school when I hear my teacher call my name, do I...
a. Excuse myself and see what she wants.
b. Finish what I was saying before I go to her.
c. Ask my friends to walk with me so we can continue the conversation.
d. Go to her depending on my mood and how I feel about her.
e. Pretend I did not hear and hide.

4. I need to work on my project, and the sign on the computer lab door says "No one allowed inside without adult supervision." I check inside but the attendant is on a break, do I...
a. Leave and come back later when the attendant may be inside.
b. Wait until the lab attendant returns but let him know how very annoyed I am because I had to wait.
c. Go inside but only spend a few minutes.

How Obedient Are You?

d.   Take my friend with me because she's a couple of months older (that's good enough, right?).

e.   Duck inside the lab when no one is looking.

5. A prefect at my school told me to allow a younger student to go ahead of me in the cafeteria line…

a.   I immediately comply.

b.   I do what they say if they're my friends (or I like them).

c.   It depends on what mood I'm in.

d.   I look at them (they can't tell me what to do).

e.   Tell her no because I have been standing in line for ten minutes and everyone needs to wait their turn.

Scoring:

Mostly As: You're Esther. You understand that rules are meant to be followed and show respect to those in authority.

Mostly Bs: You need a bit more practice if you're going to be royal. Remember that our obedience to those set in authority over us help us to be more obedient to God. Also our attitude counts for a lot.

Mostly Cs: Royalty is about doing what needs to be done—or what you're asked to do—regardless of the mood you're in. Or, how you feel about the person who asked you.

Mostly Ds: Obedience is a big part of being a queen-in-training. You will be faced with choices every day and will need to decide if getting your way is worth alienating others or displeasing God.

Mostly Es: Uh-oh! Are you Vashti? While we may not always agree with the instructions we receive, it's important for us to practice obedience. It may be a case of life or death.

2. Be willing to accept the advice of others—though Hegai was a eunuch, Esther accepted his suggestions. You may wonder what was wrong with Hegai. In Persian culture, eunuchs were considered a sub-form of humanity. They were usually captives who had been castrated at a young age. They would never have children which were one of the marks of virility in Persian culture. For Persians, the more children—especially sons—a man had, the more prestige he had. The king sent presents annually to the men who had the most children. A man who could never have children was considered less than a man[2].

Yet Esther deferred to him. She showed him respect and did exactly as he advised. No wonder Hegai was pleased with her. I imagine the other women took everything they could carry with them as they went to meet the king. It was the custom of the time that a woman could ask for anything she wanted before she went to the king's bed (Esther 2:13). I'm sure many of them requested costly items such as jewelry and items of clothing.

3. Be humble and submissive—as we read more of Esther's story, her humility and submissiveness become more apparent. As Western women, we are taught that submission and humility are signs of weakness. That's not true. Humility is not allowing people to take advantage of you or giving in to people who are "better than we are" as we sometimes interpret it. Rather, humility is showing grace and kindness to each person regardless of who they are.

The apostle Paul had this to say about humility:

Don't be selfish; don't try to impress others. Be humble, thinking of others as better than yourselves. Don't look out only for your own interests, but take an interest in others, too.

You must have the same attitude that Christ Jesus had.

Though he was God,
he did not think of equality with God
as something to cling to.
Instead, he gave up his divine privileges;
he took the humble position of a slave
and was born as a human being.
When he appeared in human form,
he humbled himself in obedience to God
and died a criminal's death on a cross.
Therefore, God elevated him to the place of highest honor
and gave him the name above all other names,
that at the name of Jesus every knee should bow,
in heaven and on earth and under the earth,
and every tongue declare that Jesus Christ is Lord,
to the glory of God the Father (Philippians 2:3–11 NLT).

Jesus was humble and we ought to be like Him. Just think about it: what could be more humble than the King of the universe coming to live on earth as a commoner, to be beaten, spat on and hung on a cross—the death reserved for the most disgusting of criminals? If Jesus hadn't been humble, He wouldn't have become the most exalted Person. He wouldn't be the Person who sits on the right hand of God (Revelation 3:21). And His name would have no power (Acts 4:12). That's why the Bible says:

Humble yourselves, therefore, under the mighty hand of God so that at the proper time he may exalt you (1 Peter 5:6 ESV).

Are you humble? Do you put the needs of others ahead of your own? Or, do you instead exalt yourself above those whom you consider to be beneath you?

Esther was taken to see the king four years after Vashti deposal. I imagine that Xerxes was refreshed by a woman who was beautiful and humble. Esther's humility was rewarded when Xerxes made her queen.

Now the king was attracted to Esther more than to any of the other women, and she won his favor and approval more than any of the other virgins. So he set a royal crown on her head and made her queen instead of Vashti (Esther 2:17 NIV).

Humility, obedience, submission and accepting the advice of others are choices we have to make. You may not have done a great job of any of these things in the past, but today you can make a choice. So, what decisions are you going to make—do you want to please the king? Or will you continue to do what you've always done?

Things I Can Do to Please God

....

....

....

....

....

....

....

....

....

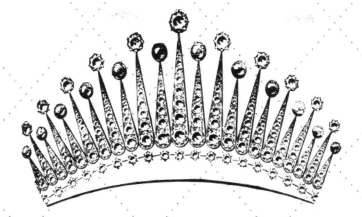

How We Treat Others

"*Treat people how you want to be treated
instead of how they treat you.*"

— Kristin Michelle Elizabeth

4

The Importance of Respect

*H*as someone ever taken credit for work you had done? How did it make you feel? In Esther chapter two, we see an example of how to handle situations where someone does something worthwhile. As you read the account in Esther 2:19–23, you'll notice that some time had passed since the king had chosen his new queen.

Mordecai sat at the king's gate. Now to us that seems idle. We may wonder why Mordecai didn't find a job so he could take care of himself. Well, he was working. In Persian culture, officers of the court remained at the gate of the palace until they were called and sent on an errand[1].

While at his position, Mordecai discovered a plot to assassinate the king. Being an honorable man, he quickly notified Esther. Mordecai would not have had direct access to the queen, so it's likely he got assistance from one of the eunuchs who had access to the harem. But why didn't Mordecai approach the king himself? Think about it for a second, if you overheard that someone was planning to kill the ruler of your country would you be able to get to him?

He's probably always surrounded by a wall of bodyguards and there's an entire book written on how to get an audience with him. It was something like that and a little more dangerous. If someone attempted to approach the king without permission, it could result in his death unless the king granted him favor as we will see in Esther 4:11.

But the queen—especially a fairly new queen—would be able to reach the king. So Mordecai used the resources that he had. Esther saw this as an opportunity to present Mordecai in a good light. She didn't say, "I have uncovered a plot against you." She said, "It has come to my attention that there is a plot against your life. It was told to me by Mordecai, the Jew." Up to that point, she had not disclosed her nationality (Esther 2:20) and she didn't reveal it then.

An investigation was done. The two men were found guilty and impaled on poles. This was a particularly gruesome way to execute those who ran amok of the government. They were fastened on sharped sticks and left to die. This was done publicly so that anyone who was thinking of rebelling against the monarchy would have a reminder of what happened to those who were found guilty[2].

Mordecai's actions were documented in the books of the chronicles of the king. Persian kings kept a record of the highlights of their life. Each entry had to be approved by the king[3]. Mordecai's name would also have been added to the list of "Royal Benefactors" who were basically persons who had done something of value for the king. At some point—months or years later—the king would reward them for their service[4].

The Bible has a lot to say about giving honor where it is due. This should be done regardless of the person's station or ours. Let's talk some more about whom we should honor and how that may look.

What it means to show honor

The word honor has several layers of meaning so we will look at each of them.

When we honor someone, we show them respect or great esteem. Showing respect can be as simple as saying "Good morning" or "Good night" and using other courtesy words at the appropriate time or being obedient.

When we respect someone, we look up to them and speak highly of them. We show our respect by the way we treat them. When we honor something, we regard it as a rare opportunity and a privilege.

Honor your parents

What does it mean to honor your parents? It may appear as though half the time our parents don't know what they're talking about. I used to feel that way too. But it seemed the older I was, the more my parents made sense. Regardless of our opinion of our parents, this is what the Bible tells us:

"Honor your father and your mother, that your days may be long in the land that the Lord your God is giving you" (Exodus 20:12 ESV).

This commandment was given to the Israelites and had a promise attached: "obey your parents and have a long life". So, let me ask you: if the length of your life was based on how you treat your parents today, would you have a long life?

Are you honoring your parents by showing them the proper respect? How do you speak to them? Do you use an appropriate tone? Do your words show how you feel about them?

Do you appreciate the gift of your parents? Most of us know someone who is from a single parent family or who has absent parents. We may even know persons who are orphans. When we are feeling unhappy about something our parents have said or done, we may think that person is lucky—at least, luckier than we are. But is that really the truth?

Would you truly want to be free of your parents? I understand that some of you may have parents who are abusive—I am so sorry about that—but if that's your situation I hope you have someone who fills the role of a parent for you. Would your life truly be better without this person who gives you advice and takes care of you?

When we honor something or someone, we fulfill an obligation or keep an agreement. What are some of the obligations we have to our parents?

'Honor your father and mother. Love your neighbor as yourself.'

- Matthew 19:19 NLT

Obligated to obey

As children, we have an obligation to obey and to respect our parents.

Children, obey your parents in the Lord, for this is right. "Honor your father and mother" (this is the first commandment with a promise), "that it may go well with you and that you may live long in the land". Fathers, do not provoke your children to anger, but bring them up in the discipline and instruction of the Lord (Ephesians 6:1–4 ESV).

I know you're probably focusing on the phrase "Fathers, do not provoke your children to anger" and thinking "See, my parents shouldn't provoke me to anger". And you would be right, parents shouldn't exasperate their children—by that we mean parents shouldn't deliberately try to provoke their children to anger.

It does not mean that their actions won't result in their children becoming annoyed or even angry, but it does mean they shouldn't do things deliberately to make their child angry. But even if they provoke you to anger, you're expected to obey them. It may not seem fair but remember each of us will one day have to answer to God for our own actions—even our parents.

Obligated to accept discipline

At the same time, parents have the right to discipline their children and instruct them about worldly and godly things. Children have an obligation to be disciplined and to accept the instructions given by their parents.

The idea of discipline is one that is addressed many times in Scripture. Here are a few more instances:

A rod and a reprimand impart wisdom,
but a child left undisciplined disgraces its mother (Proverbs 29:15 NIV).

A child who is not disciplined goes on to disgrace her mother. It means therefore that we are honor-bound to make our parents proud. Or, at least not behave in such a way that we disgrace them.

Do not withhold discipline from a child; if you strike him with a rod, he will not die. If you strike him with the rod, you will save his soul from Sheol (Proverbs 23:13-14 ESV).

God wants us to treat each other with love and respect.

This is not an invitation for children to be physically abused. Rather, it was an admonishment that children should not be allowed to have their way in everything because to do so would be to raise them without direction. Think about it for a second: do you know someone who had been given everything they wanted? Someone who had no restrictions, or rules and their parent never seemed to discipline them? What would you say about that person's character? Do they respect others? Do they treat people with respect?

I have met persons who did not receive any parental discipline. They were typically rude and entitled. They thought they should be allowed to have their way in everything and with everyone. That is not what God intended for anyone. You see, God wants us to treat each other with love and respect. A person who is given their way in everything does not usually learn to respect the desires and feelings of others. King Xerxes may have been one such person. The book of Esther portrays him as a man who made rash decisions without considering the needs of others (more on that later).

I know being disciplined is hard. It can feel as though we have no rights and that our needs do not matter, but we can take hope from the following verses:

And have you completely forgotten this word of encouragement that addresses you as a father addresses his son? It says,
"My son, do not make light of the Lord's discipline,
    and do not lose heart when he rebukes you,
because the Lord disciplines the one he loves,
    and he chastens everyone he accepts as his son."

Endure hardship as discipline; God is treating you as his children. For what children are not disciplined by their father? If you are not disciplined—and everyone undergoes discipline—then you are not legitimate, not true sons and daughters at all. Moreover, we have all had human fathers who disciplined us and we respected them for it. How much more should we submit to the Father of spirits and live! They disciplined us for a little while as they thought best; but God disciplines us for our good, in order that we may share in his holiness. No discipline seems pleasant at the time, but painful. Later on, however, it produces a harvest of righteousness and peace for those who have been trained by it (Hebrews 12:5–11 NIV).

Our parents discipline us because they love us. They want us to develop a character that will serve us later in life. If we are petulant, moody and sullen, we will have difficulties at school and later in the working world. Our parents discipline us so we can learn how to follow authority. This advice will be needed as long as we are alive because there is always someone in authority over us—teachers, government officials, employers, etc. Ultimately, we learn to obey so we can obey God.

Obligated to accept instructions

If your parents are anything like mine you would have heard this phrase (or some variation of it) a thousand times:

Train up a child in the way he should go; even when he is old he will not depart from it (Proverbs 22:6 ESV).

Parents have an obligation to teach their children how to behave in a manner which brings glory to God. Children are obliged to accept this instruction. The Israelites were charged to pass on the instructions on how to obey God to their children. They were told to talk about it at various times during their day—at mealtimes, while doing chores and at bedtime.

And you must commit yourselves wholeheartedly to these commands that I am giving you today. Repeat them again and again to your children. Talk about them when you are at home and when you are on the road, when you are going to bed and when you are getting up (Deuteronomy 6:6–7 NLT).

If you've ever wondered why your parents tell you the same things over and over, this is the reason. Have you ever noticed that when someone wants you to remember something they repeat it many times? Or have you ever tried to memorize something, like the lyrics of a song? The more you listen to it, the more it sticks in your brain.

Being a parent is a little bit like that—instructions have to be repeated many times before they register—and stick—in our brains. When it is repeated often, we begin to understand that it's something that's important to our parents and need to be listened to. As King Solomon puts it:

> Hear, my son, your father's instruction,
> and forsake not your mother's teaching,
> for they are a graceful garland for your head
> and pendants for your neck (Proverbs 1:8–9 ESV).

Let us learn to heed the instructions of our parents and treat them like our favorite accessories and keep them with us at all times.

Our obligation to our parents may be summed up in this verse:

> Children, obey your parents in everything, for this pleases the Lord (Colossians 3:20 ESV).

When we obey our parents, we please God. Will it always be easy? No, but it is the right thing to do. Even more important, it's what God desires.

Obey the law

Rulers—we don't always believe that our leaders are making the right decision but we are honor-bound to obey the law. As queens-in-training, we have to learn to obey the laws of the land regardless of our personal opinions.

Everyone must submit to governing authorities. For all authority comes from God, and those in positions of authority have been placed there by God. So anyone who rebels against authority is rebelling against what God has instituted, and they will be punished. For the authorities do not strike fear in people who are doing right, but in those who are doing wrong. Would you like to live without fear of the authorities? Do what is right, and they will honor you. The authorities are God's servants, sent for your good. But if you are doing wrong, of course you should be afraid, for they have the power to punish you. They are God's servants, sent for the very purpose of punishing those who do what is wrong. So you must submit to them, not only to avoid punishment, but also to keep a clear conscience.

Pay your taxes, too, for these same reasons. For government workers need to be paid. They are serving God in what they do. Give to everyone what you owe them: Pay your taxes and government fees to those who collect them, and give respect and honor to those who are in authority (Romans 13:1–7 NLT).

Wow! Those are a lot of instructions, so let me break it down:

- Obey your rulers because they were put in charge by God.
- When we rebel against our leaders, we're really rebelling against God.

- Pay your taxes so that the government workers can be paid.

When there are so many stories of corruption in government we may wonder why we should pay our taxes since the money probably won't get to the right place anyway. Even if our taxes are not used for the intended purpose, we need to pay them as required by law. We are responsible for our obedience; let the dishonest steward answer to God for his own actions. But let us remain faithful and do the right thing.

Respect the elderly

Elderly People—we should show respect to those who are older than we are. The elderly have a lot of advice to give, so we should take the time to learn from them. A few caveats: not every elderly person is wise. Still, we can show them respect by being courteous and by respecting the fact that they are older than us. There are many simple ways in which we can show respect to our elders:

- By not speaking when they are.
- By offering them our seat if there is none available.
- By doing small chores and errands for them.

"You shall stand up before the gray head and honor the face of an old man, and you shall fear your God: I am the Lord" (Leviticus 19:32 ESV).

As we show respect to our elders, we acknowledge that we fear God—not in a sense of being afraid of Him—but in the sense that we give Him reverence and honor due to Him.

Respect masters

Bondservants, obey your earthly masters with fear and trembling, with a sincere heart, as you would Christ, not by the way of eye-service, as people-pleasers, but as bondservants of Christ, doing the will of God from the heart, rendering service with a good will as to the Lord and not to man, knowing that whatever good anyone does, this he will receive back from the Lord, whether he is a bondservant or is free (Ephesians 6:5–8 ESV).

As children, it can seem as though we have a lot of masters—older siblings, parents, teachers and other family members. In fact, anyone who is older seems to want to boss you around. I know the feeling and it never really goes away. As an adult, there are also persons whom we have to show respect to parents, employers, authority figures and anyone who is older than we are. I say this not to diminish the way you are feeling but to quantify it: there's always someone to who respect must be given.

I think God designed it that way. In His perfect model, He wants each person to give the respect he would want for himself to every man. We were created to reverence God. It becomes easier to show reverence to our Heavenly Father if we have already mastered the art of showing respect to other persons.

Respect Peers

I can almost see your expression: "Surely she can't mean that I am to obey and respect persons who are the same age I am?" Well, let me ask you a question: "Do you want people to respect you?" I'm sure your answer is yes. Everyone wants to be treated with respect—and not just by persons who are younger than we are.

Even though someone may be your age or younger, you still need to respect them. Does it mean that you do everything they say? Not necessarily. You will have to learn how to weigh the words and instructions given to us by our peers. Do not do things that will get us into trouble with our parents or other authority figures. Do not do things that bring dishonor or shame to other persons. For example, if your classmates are teasing a student because they may look or act different than everyone else, do not join in.

Showing respect to our peers means speaking to them in a manner and tone that acknowledges them as human beings—persons created by God in His image and for His purpose. God created you because He had a plan for your life. He also created that person because He had a plan for their life (Jeremiah 1:9). God does not treat that person any differently (Job 34:19), why should you?

Do not withhold good from those to whom it is due,
When it is in your power to do it (Proverbs 3:27 ESV).

70

As children, we sometimes feel as though we are powerless—here is something you can do: as queens-in-training, you can treat everyone with respect. Learn to love them as Christ loves you and honor them as you would want to be honored. But do it without expecting anything in return. Do it even if they don't treat you with the same respect.

Be devoted to one another in love. Honor one another above yourselves (Romans 12:10 NIV).

Respect God

I deliberately left this one for last, not because it's the least important, but because it is the *most* important. And also because our ability to honor God is somewhat dependent on our ability to honor parents, peers and other authority figures.

When we are born, we are entrusted into a family either biological or otherwise. This family unit is responsible for teaching us the necessary social skills so that we can move on to the next sphere of learning: school. In school, we learn more about the government, how it functions and how to respect its officials and our environments.

The roles of parents and teachers overlap but by the time we get to a particular age, we are expected to function at a certain level. We should be able to follow simple and complex instructions. We are trained to be good citizens. Some of the responsibilities of a good citizen are:

- Pay his/her share of tax that is levied for the good of the community.
- Obey the laws of the land.
- Participate in the democratic process.
- Respect the rights, beliefs, and opinions of others[5].

As queens-in-training, we honor each person as though we were giving honor unto God. But more importantly, we honor God by doing as He commands. Let it not be said about us:

For although they knew God, they did not honor him as God or give thanks to him, but they became futile in their thinking, and their foolish hearts were darkened (Romans 1:21 ESV).

WE WERE *created* to *revere God.*

5

Creating A Culture of Care

When you read about Jesus in the New Testament, one thing that stands out is His compassion. Unlike the rulers of the time, Jesus was able to see past a person's background or financial capacity to their true need. His compassion motivated Him to heal the sick, feed the hungry, preach the gospel and meet the people's need for social interaction (Luke 4:18). Jesus felt pity for the people because He saw their needs and empathized with them. Do you think King Xerxes had a lot of compassion on the Jews?

Let's revisit Esther 3. Haman had offered the king an exorbitant sum of money for the Jews destruction. His reason was the very flimsy excuse that they did not follow the king's laws. There was no investigation or questions asked. The king agreed to have the people destroyed and refused to accept the money. Let's recap some of the things that happened in Xerxes' reign:

- There had been a 180-day banquet during which the king had "displayed the vast wealth of his kingdom and the splendor and glory of his majesty" (Esther 1:4 NIV).
- There had been a seven-day feast with no expenses spared (Esther 1:5).
- An expedition to procure, house, feed and keep an untold number of virgins had taken place (Esther 2:2-4).
- King Xerxes had mounted a costly and unsuccessful campaign against Greece.
- There had been a wedding feast during which time the king had given lavish gifts, including, some scholars believe, a cessation of taxes (Esther 2:18).

Given the amount of funds that had been spent in about four years, I can understand why Haman offered to pay such a ridiculous sum of money. He had hoped to tempt the king with the possibility of at least partially replenishing his coffers. The Bible records the king's refusal to accept the funds, but it's possible the story didn't end there.

"Keep the money," the king said to Haman, "and do with the people as you please" (Esther 3:11 NIV).

Eastern societies practice polite refusal as part of their bargaining process. The person who makes an offer continues to do so even after refusal until the other person politely accepts[1]. The king may have agreed to the massacre because of the money Haman promised to pay.

The edicts were written and, "spurred on by the king", the couriers leave with their missives of death (Esther 3:15). The town is perplexed but Haman and the king sit down to drink. Did you find it strange that after Xerxes and Haman sent out the decree which called for the extinction of an entire nation they started drinking? Let me explain the reason behind that strange action.

Persians made decisions when they were drunk. If they happened to make a decision when they were sober, they would actually get drunk and revisit the idea to see if they still liked it. If they liked it while they were sober as well as drunk, they kept it[2]. In this case, it was more of a celebration. A new decision could not be made since the decree had already been sent out and could not be repealed.

Xerxes' actions did not reflect a ruler who had compassion on his people. Quite the contrary, his actions—and words—suggested "I couldn't care less". As representatives of Christ, we should feel compassion for the people around us—even the ones we don't like very much. We express our compassion in words and actions. Think about your last 24 hours. Were there any opportunities for you to show compassion to anyone? Did you treat them as Jesus would want you to? Or, did you callously disregard their need?

Ways I can show compassion:

....

....

....

....

....

....

....

....

....

A culture of care

As queens-in-training, we need to cultivate a culture of care. I can see you rolling your eyes. What exactly is a culture of care? Basically, it should be our personal agenda to show care and compassion to everyone we meet. Ralph Waldo Emerson once said:

"Sow a thought and you reap an action; sow an act and you reap a habit; sow a habit and you reap a character; sow a character and you reap a destiny."

I want us to take it one step further: sow a character, reap a culture. For this example and the rest of this book, culture is the way we behave and treat others because of our beliefs. We become what we think about. Oh, you may not realize it but the things that engage your thought will eventually be reflected in your behavior and demeanor.

If you think someone is stupid, eventually you will start to treat them that way. They way you speak to and about them will reflect what you think of them. So, if we want to treat people with compassion we have to actually care about them.

You're probably thinking you can't care about every single person on the planet especially if you've never met them. But we are called to love all people. This is what Jesus told His disciples:

"A new commandment I give to you, that you love one another; as I have loved you, that you also love one another. By this all will know that you are My disciples, if you have love for one another" (John 13:34-35 NKJV).

Jesus knew this was one of the hardest things He could ask His disciples to do. Yet nothing will quite testify of Him as much as this one thing. Think about it for a second: I'm sure you've had teachers whom you prefer over others. Why do you like that teacher? Could it be because he or she has displayed care, maybe even love, towards you? Do you find yourself willing to work a little harder or do a little more to please that teacher?

I've had teachers like that—people who encouraged me to do more, who inspired me to dig a little deeper. Teachers like that motivate students to change the world—at least their little part of it.

What if you could emulate that caring attitude with everyone you meet? And before you tell me it's impossible, let me remind you of your favorite teacher again: are you the only person who is treated with favor? She's probably been teaching for a long time and has met many students. I'm certain you are not the first student who has considered her your favorite. She has created a culture of care, one that is demonstrated by the way she treats all her students.

How to Create a Culture of Care

So just how do we create a culture of care? It starts with our focus. Are you focused more on one-upping your fellow man than on Christ? Until we make Jesus our priority, we will likely struggle to care about others. Hebrews 12:2 encourages us to fix our eyes on Jesus who is the author and finisher of our faith.

In other words, let's focus on Christ who lived and died as the perfect example. If He could do surrounded by people who hated and eventually killed Him, we can do it too.

As we focus on Christ, we take on His character and learn to love others. Even when we don't understand them or like the things they do. We treat them with compassion, doing things for their benefit.

Let's fast-forward to Esther 4. Mordecai, who lived in the city of Susa, was one of the first persons to hear the decree. He was perplexed and tormented. The king had given his neighbors the right to kill him without cause. All the Jews in the Persian Empire would be destroyed.

Think about it for a second: for one day the people of Media-Persia could kill anyone as long as they were a Jew. They would be allowed to take what was called the spoils of war—so anything of value would be taken by the person who killed you. If this happened today, it would mean the person who killed you could take all your possessions.

Mordecai went to the king's gate wearing grain cloth and ashes. He wailed and moaned and made a big commotion. Though Esther was in the palace, she had not heard what was going on until Mordecai gave her the information. When Esther heard that her cousin was outside and the way he was dressed she was concerned. First of all, he wouldn't be able to go beyond the king's gate as that wasn't allowed (Esther 4:2). Secondly, Jews only wore sackcloth and ashes when they were in deep distress or to signal deep humiliation[3].

Thirdly, she knew that something was seriously wrong because of how Mordecai was dressed on that particular day.

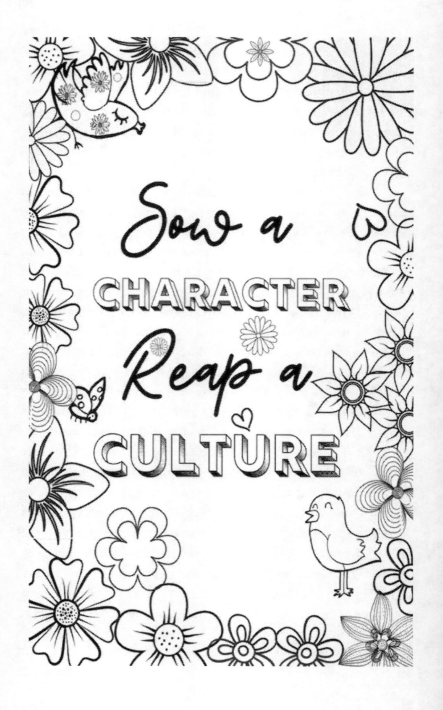

The edicts went out on the thirteenth day of the month of Nisan which is the first month of the Jewish calendar. In a few hours, they would be celebrating the Passover. Hundreds of years earlier, they had been delivered from their Egyptian captors by Jehovah. You can read that account in Exodus 12. Each year, the Passover was celebrated in remembrance of their deliverance.

On the tenth day of Nisan, they would have taken the Passover lamb. It would have been killed at twilight and eaten on the fourteenth day of Nisan (Exodus 14:3–7). It was to be a day of celebration, not humiliation or mourning. But Mordecai told an unbelievable tale. They were to be murdered. The king had signed their death sentence.

Esther demonstrated affection for Mordecai. She tried to provide him with proper attire so that he could occupy his position at the king's gate. Then, she tried to find out the cause of his agitation. She couldn't speak to him directly but she sent someone he trusted and would confide in. You may argue that Mordecai was family and had to be treated with care. Yes, you are correct. But you see my dear queen-in-training, a culture of care begins at home. Too many times we fail to treat the members of our family with the respect and care they deserve or that God requires.

In Esther 2, we saw Mordecai walking back and forth near the courtyard of the harem to find out how Esther was and what was happening to her. He had already shown how much he cared for his young cousin by adopting her and raising her as his daughter, but there was another aspect of his concern.

As a Jewess, it was forbidden for Esther to marry a non-Jew. God had warned the Israelites against intermarrying centuries before as He had known it would lead to idolatry[4]. Yet, as a subordinate people, there was nothing Esther or Mordecai could have done to prevent her from being taken to the king's harem. Once she was inside the palace, Esther had no contact with the outside world.

The truth of it was, even if there was something wrong with Esther, he couldn't storm the castle and demand that she be taken care of. He couldn't pull her from the harem and take her home. The only thing he could do was pray for her (and maybe tried to influence the eunuchs to take care of her for him). Still, Mordecai continued to care for her. Because you see, the book of Esther is about family—not just the ones we're related to by blood, but the ones we're connected to by heart. How well do you care for your family? Do they know you care? How do you show it?

The family unit is diverse and unique and we have an obligation to our relatives. Unfortunately, the family is not always the safe haven God intended for it to be. God designed the family as the place where we learn to care about each other and Him. We learn compassion for fellow human beings.

As the king, Xerxes should have felt compassion for all the peoples in his land. He should never have agreed to the annihilation of the Jews simply because his favored prince Haman had requested it. Like Esther, he should have taken steps to get to the bottom of the problem.

Mordecai wanted Esther to go into the king to request the reversal of the command. At first, Esther was hesitant. She knew she couldn't just walk in to see the king. He was her husband but it wasn't a modern marriage. They were separated by hundreds of years of traditions and practices. It had been 30 days since the king had requested to see her. If she went in to see him without being summoned, she could lose her life.

God always takes care of His people.

Mordecai reminded her that God always takes care of His people. He also pointed out that she may have been chosen as the queen to save her people. Mordecai told Esther something each of us needs to know: God has a plan for our lives. We may not see it, but He does. And the plan He has for us is bigger than anything we can accomplish on our own. That's why as queens-in-training we have to lean heavily on our Heavenly Father. We should spend time in Bible study, prayer and fasting.

Before she intervened for her people, Esther asked Mordecai to tell the Jews in Susa to go without food or drink for three days. On a normal day, fasting is a big deal. But on the day before the Passover, it was monumental. Jews always kept the Passover unless they were unclean. If they were unclean, the Passover was deferred one month and kept then (Numbers 9:6–13). Mordecai and the Jews in Susa agreed to forgo the Passover celebration because they wanted God to intervene on their behalf.

There will be times in your life when you need God to intervene on your behalf. Sometimes just praying may be enough. But other times you may have to give up something to show God how serious you are about whatever it is that you desire. What are you willing to sacrifice?

Can you give up food for a few hours or days? Are you willing to forgo your screen time or recreational phone use? Please bear in mind that we can't bribe God—there's nothing we can do to compel Him to do things that He would not ordinarily do. But we can show Him how much we desire His intervention by our actions. Esther was willing to give up her life for her people. Is there anything, or anyone, you're willing to die for? (We'll talk more about prayer and fasting later.)

Compassion leads to service which almost always involves sacrifice. Having compassion for someone is not enough. It should compel you to take some form of action. You may already be familiar with the story of the Good Samaritan, but let's look at it together:

On one occasion an expert in the law stood up to test Jesus. "Teacher," he asked, "what must I do to inherit eternal life?"

"What is written in the Law?" he replied. "How do you read it?"

He answered, "'Love the Lord your God with all your heart and with all your soul and with all your strength and with all your mind'; and, 'Love your neighbor as yourself.'"

"You have answered correctly," Jesus replied. "Do this and you will live."

But he wanted to justify himself, so he asked Jesus, "And who is my neighbor?"

In reply Jesus said: "A man was going down from Jerusalem to Jericho, when he was attacked by robbers. They stripped him of his clothes, beat him and went away, leaving him half dead. A priest happened to be going down the same road, and when he saw the man, he passed by on the other side. So too, a Levite, when he came to the place and saw him, passed by on the other side. But a Samaritan, as he traveled, came where the man was; and when he saw him, he took pity on him. He went to him and bandaged his wounds, pouring on oil and wine. Then he put the man on his own donkey, brought him to an inn and took care of him. The next day he took out two denarii and gave them to the innkeeper. 'Look after him,' he said, 'and when I return, I will reimburse you for any extra expense you may have.'

"Which of these three do you think was a neighbor to the man who fell into the hands of robbers?"

The expert in the law replied, "The one who had mercy on him."

Jesus told him, "Go and do likewise" (Luke 10:25–37 NIV).

Jesus identified three categories of people in his parable: a priest, a Levite, and a Samaritan. This was deliberate. The Levites had the responsibility to care for the Temple and the things related to worship and to God. The priests were from the tribe of Levi. They were responsible for offering sacrifices for the sins of the Israelites. Basically, his job description was to care for all people (Numbers 3:5-13, 1 Chronicles 9:17-34).

The original Greek word translated as a priest in that passage is hiereús (pronounced hee-er-yooce') and could also mean high priest[5]. The high priest was a descendant of Aaron. He had the awesome duty of being the only person who could go into the Most Holy place of the Temple and atone for the sins of the people (Leviticus 16).

If this were today, we could say the priests were like the pastors and elders of the church responsible for teaching the people about God and how to serve Him. The high priest would be like Jesus who mediates for us and stands between our sin and the Heavenly Father. This was a huge role.

The Samaritans and the Jews were bitter rivals. Jews did not mingle with Samarians or vice versa. Interestingly, they were all descendants of Abraham. By the time Jesus came, they had spent hundreds of years locked in opposition. When the lawyer started the discourse with Jesus, he wanted to know how he could get to heaven. Maybe he secretly thought Jesus would tell him he was already on his way because of how well he kept the commandments. He was in for a surprise.

Jesus immediately turned his attention to the underlying threads which bound the Ten Commandments together: love for God and love for one's neighbor. This opened a huge debate for His audience: who was your neighbor? I bet even knowing the answer given by Christ you'd probably describe your neighbor as the person living nearest to you. Jesus' parable highlighted the fact that sometimes the people who are expected to care don't. And the ones we believe to be our enemies can depict a more caring attitude towards us.

We can say we care but our actions will reveal the truth. The Samaritan took pity on the injured man even though he was a Jew. The Samaritan could have said, "One of his own people will soon pass by and help him. Besides, I'm very busy. I don't have time to stop."

That's how we behave sometimes. We feel pity for someone, but we allow the noise of our lives to drown it out. Until our compassion compels us to help where there is a need, it's not enough to change our characters because we're not demonstrating a culture of care.

As queens-in-training, our compassion should be engrained in our nature. It should compel us to service. Showing compassion does not always require grandiose actions. It can be as simple as listening to a friend or classmate who had a bad experience. Or, offering to help someone who needs it.

God created us to experience a depth of emotion. When we tap into it, we become forces for change and can have huge impacts on the lives of the people around us. When we turn it off by ignoring our conscience, we can do unimaginable evil.

God has gifted you with the ability to change the world you live in. But you have to decide: do you want to make life better for the people around you? Or, do you want to pursue selfish habits to improve your life regardless of the cost?

If the Good Samaritan had ignored the injured man in pursuit of his goals, the man would have died. Instead, something positive happened because one man took the time to care for his neighbor. What do you think happened when the man woke up and remembered what had happened to him? Let's imagine the end of that story.

His head hurt. He had been travelling from Jerusalem. Where had he been going? Why was it so hard to remember? Jericho! He had been going to Jericho. And then...what happened after that? Adonai, why can't I remember?

Right. He had been attacked. Three men...or was it four had jumped out at him just as he reached the canyon. They had beaten him...no wonder everything was sore. They had taken his camel and everything he had. Where was he? And why wasn't he dead?

"Oh, you're awake." Her voice was cheerful and loud. He turned his head in the direction from which the sound came but she had opened the door and brought with her the light. He shut his eyes in defense as the miners in his head intensified their efforts.

A cool rag was placed on his head and over his eyes. The pounding in his head responded by dialing down a tiny bit.

"Where am I?" His voice was raspy, his throat sore.

"You're in Jericho."

Jericho? He had been nowhere near his destination when he'd been attacked.

> *Until our compassion compels us to help where there is a need, it's not enough to change our characters.*

"How—?"

"A businessman from Samaria passed you on the road. You had been badly beaten and left for dead. He did what he could for you and brought you here. He left some money to cover your expenses and will pay the rest when he returns in a few days."

A Samaritan had helped him?

Do you think that Jew had the same view of Samaritans going forward? I don't think so. More than likely he would have revised his opinion as he realized what he had thought of the Samaritans had been the result of years of prejudice. As queens-in-training, we have a choice to make. Will we be agents of change or of destruction? You choose.

Like the Good Samaritan, Esther chose to serve her people. She could have told Mordecai "Sorry, Cousin, I'm not going to risk my life for the Jews. You told me not to reveal my identity and I didn't, so no one knows who I am. Besides, the king favors me. He chose me over all the other virgins. I'll take my chance." But she didn't. She allowed her compassion to compel her to take action but she knew she couldn't do it alone.

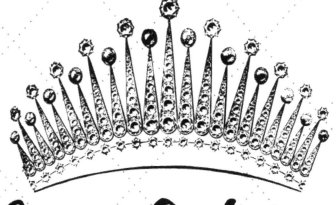

My Actions Matter

"*Act as if what you do makes a difference. It does.*"

— William James

6

Our Actions Matter

*I*n Esther 3, we uncover another one of Haman's dangerous traits: the ability to twist words. Mordecai had refused to bow down before him and excused himself by explaining that he was a Jew. I imagine Haman did some research to figure out why being a Jew exempted Mordecai from bowing before him.

During the course of his investigation, he learned that the Jews served a different God than the ones his people served. Jews did not bow down before or worship idols. Maybe he read about Daniel who had been thrown into the lions' den because he continued to pray to his God despite King Darius' edict[1].

Or, he had heard about Shadrach, Meshach, and Abed-Nego who had been thrown into the fiery furnace when they did not bow down before Nebuchadnezzar's golden statue[2]. He should have learned that the unseen God of these four Hebrew boys—the same God worshipped by Mordecai—had delivered them in amazing ways. But he didn't get the lesson. He didn't realize that the Hebrew God was powerful and able to save. Maybe he thought it was just coincidence. Haman may have noticed that three kings had issued irreversible edicts regarding worship but the Jewish people refused to obey.

Instead of telling King Xerxes that the Jews had unusual beliefs about who could be worshipped, he said they refused to obey all his laws. He hinted to the king that there was a threat of insurgent from a certain group of people who were dispersed throughout his kingdom. Haman did this without being specific about the peoples' nationality.

"There is a certain people scattered and dispersed among the people in all the provinces of your kingdom; their laws are different from all other people's, and they do not keep the king's laws. Therefore it is not fitting for the king to let them remain" (Esther 3:8 NKJV).

If an entire nation of people refused to obey every law of the kingdom wouldn't the king have known about it? Xerxes did not analyze Haman's word. He accepted it as truth and condemned an entire nationality of people to death.

It could be that Haman spoke strategically because he knew that a few years earlier King Xerxes had fought several revolts in Egypt and Babylon[3].

As queens-in-training, learn to speak the truth at all times and to analyze the words (and actions) of the people around you so you can discern truth from lies. Speaking the truth is necessary because the One whom we represent is Truth. It won't always be easy to speak the truth; sometimes a lie seems easier (especially if it will prevent us from getting into

You have to decide: is sinning against God worth doing something that seems easy, or fun.

trouble). But at some point, you have to decide: is sinning against God worth doing something that seems easy, or fun?

Joseph had to make a similar choice. We read his story in Genesis 39. He had been sold into slavery by his brothers and became the house manager for an Egyptian named Potiphar. He attracted the attention of Potiphar's wife who wanted to sleep with him. But Joseph realized if he did, he would sin against God (Genesis 39:9). When he ran away from Potiphar's wife, she accused him of rape and he was thrown in prison. Joseph was punished for doing the honorable thing.

There may be consequences for speaking the truth. But our first thought should always be how we can honor God. If you need a little more encouragement to speak the truth, here's what the Bible says about lying and those who lie:

Lying lips are an abomination to the Lord, but those who act faithfully are his delight (Proverbs 12:22 ESV).

A false witness will not go unpunished, and he who breathes out lies will perish (Proverbs 19:9 ESV).

For nothing is hidden that will not be made manifest, nor is anything secret that will not be known and come to light (Luke 8:17 ESV).

"One who is faithful in a very little is also faithful in much, and one who is dishonest in a very little is also dishonest in much" (Luke 16:10 ESV).

For "Whoever desires to love life and see good days, let him keep his tongue from evil and his lips from speaking deceit;" (1 Peter 3:10 ESV).

We may believe no one knows we're lying, but God always knows. Eventually, our lies will be revealed and we will have to bear the punishment for the lies we've told.

The more we choose to honor God with our words, the more He will trust us with things of greater responsibility. As ambassadors, we have a duty to represent the King to the best of our abilities. Let us not prove to be poor witnesses because we are unable to speak the truth.

Figure out what's right

Discernment is another skill queens-in-training need. Basically, discernment is the ability to figure out right from wrong. It's being able to sense the difference between truth and falsehood. This is an important quality for a queen to have. Let's put ourselves in King Xerxes' position for a moment.

Imagine you were the leader of a vast kingdom. You had millions of persons whose welfare depended on the decisions you made as a monarch. To carry out your functions effectively, you need to have persons who can advise you on the best course of action for the nation.

Each of your advisors has their own agenda. They were more concerned with how they could advance themselves than what was best for the country.

How would you be able to tell if the advice you received was the right thing to do? That's where discernment comes in. Being able to sense when someone is telling the truth or giving good advice will help you to make the right decisions.

You rely on this skill every day. Discernment is what happens when you sense someone is lying. Or, when you believe something is wrong even though you may not be able to explain why.

Wouldn't it be nice to know what to do in every situation? As queens-in-training, our discernment comes from the Holy Spirit.

Whether you turn to the right or to the left, your ears will hear a voice behind you, saying, "This is the way; walk in it" (Isaiah 30:21 NIV).

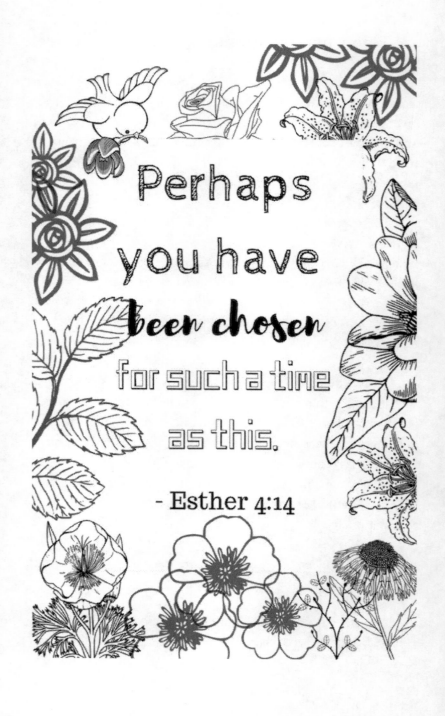

Perhaps you have been chosen for such a time as this.

- Esther 4:14

This becomes more evident the longer we spend in God's presence. As we spend time studying our Bibles and praying, we begin to sense when things are not right.

The dangers of pride and prejudice

We learn another key lesson from Haman—the dangerous effects of prejudice. In a nutshell, prejudice is a preconceived notion about someone or something. Do you know someone who dislikes all the persons of a certain profession because they had a bad experience with one? Or, maybe you know people who won't eat a particular food because they don't like how it looks. They made a judgment of the thing or person because of an idea in their head. That's what Haman did to Mordecai.

When Haman realized Mordecai would not bow down, he made the assumption that Mordecai either hated him or did not respect his position. He made no attempt to get to know Mordecai. Nor did Haman ask Mordecai for the reason behind his actions. His pride held him back.

This is what the Bible has to say about pride:

Pride goes before destruction, and a haughty spirit before a fall (Proverbs 16:18 ESV).

For if anyone thinks he is something, when he is nothing, he deceives himself (Galatians 6:3 ESV).

When pride comes, then comes disgrace, but with the humble is wisdom (Proverbs 11:2 ESV).

But he gives more grace. Therefore it says, "God opposes the proud, but gives grace to the humble" (James 4:6 ESV).

Everyone who is arrogant in heart is an abomination to the Lord; be assured, he will not go unpunished (Proverbs 16:5 ESV).

For all that is in the world—the desires of the flesh and the desires of the eyes and pride in possessions—is not from the Father but is from the world (1 John 2:16 ESV).

Now you're wondering: is pride a bad thing? Yes and no. Pride is a sense of pleasure or satisfaction that you get because you (or people you know) did or got something good. It's the sense of your own worth and respect for yourself. These are good things. But when we start to believe that we're better or more important than other people, it's not. That's the kind of pride highlighted in the verses above. The kind of pride Haman had.

When God looks at us, He doesn't see color, gender, age or any other superficial thing.

He truly believed he was better than Mordecai and deserved the adoration and exultation commanded by the king.

Let's talk about prejudice. Prejudice is an unfair and unreasonable opinion or feeling. This opinion is usually formed without enough thought or knowledge. It's judging things—or people—on the surface. Has that ever happened to you? Maybe you know someone who dislikes you for no apparent reason. Or, maybe you've disliked someone on sight without knowing why. That could be as a result of prejudice.

It's easy for us to look at a person or a thing and decide we don't like them. But as queens-in-training, God has called us to behave differently. When He looks at us, He doesn't see color, gender, age or any other superficial thing. He looks at our hearts (1 Samuel 16:7). He wants us to be like Him— loving and treating each other as we want to be treated.

Do you have too much pride?

Is your pride rising to dangerous levels?

1) I think I'm the smartest person in any gathering.

a. Never.
b. I don't worry about it much.
c. All the time.

2) My friends are lucky I hang out with them.

a. No way! I'm the one who's lucky.
b. We're all lucky.
c. That's what I tell them all the time.

3) Your parents get you a generic cell phone. Your response is...

a. Great! I needed a new phone.
b. Excitement until your friends see it, and then you feel self-conscious.
c. Shame. Everyone I know has a brand name phone; I can't let anyone see me with this.

4) Whenever I post something on social media, I...

a. Don't worry about it.
b. Scroll through my friends' feeds to see how well I'm doing compared to them.
c. I check back often to see how many likes and shares I have so I can tell everyone how popular I am on social media.

5) My friends and I are always fashionably dressed. Whenever someone who's not dressed in the latest fashion tries to join our group, I...

a. Ignore it. I'm more concerned with how the person acts than how they dress.
b. If they still look nice they can join the group.
c. Want nothing to do with them. I refuse to associate with people who don't have a good fashion sense.

Do you have too much pride?

Is your pride rising to dangerous levels?

6) Whenever I get a high score on a test...

a. Tell my family and friends so they can share in my excitement.
b. I hold my test paper so others can see my good grades.
c. Tell everyone I meet how well I'm doing in school.

7) I'm on the basketball team. At the last game I scored the most points. I...

a. Graciously accept the congratulations of my team members but remind everyone it was a team effort.
b. Beam when people congratulate me. I worked hard on my game.
c. Make note of all the persons who didn't congratulate me and approach them individually to give them the chance to congratulate me on my great game.

Scoring:

Mostly As: You understand that while it's okay to be proud of your accomplishments, it should not be used to make anyone feel bad about themselves. Each of us have different abilities and talents and should be given credit where due.

Mostly Bs: There's a very thin line between being proud of yourself and being cocky. You don't want to become boastful about what you have done. That's an easy way to isolate people.

Mostly Cs: Uh-oh! Be careful how you gloat about your accomplishments. You don't want to be like Haman whose pride caused him to make the decision to hurt Mordecai and his people. Spend some time figuring out why you want people to see your accomplishments and ask God to help you overcome the sin of pride.

7

What About Our Friends?

*J*he desire for human contact was wired into human DNA. It's how God designed us. He knew the relationships we formed with each other would affect the people we become. And so we need to think about who we allow into our circle of friends.

Choose your friends wisely

The people we surround ourselves with say a lot about who we are. They also have an impact on how we behave and the person we become. That's why we need to choose our friends wisely. In this scenario, Haman called his friends together and explained how angry he was because Mordecai refused to bow down before him. He claimed that everything he had meant nothing because of what he considered Mordecai's defiance. And look at what happened next:

His wife Zeresh and all his friends said to him, "Have a pole set up, reaching to a height of fifty cubits, and ask the king in the morning to have Mordecai impaled on it. Then go with the king to the banquet and enjoy yourself." This suggestion delighted Haman, and he had the pole set up (Esther 5:14 NIV).

A good friend would have talked him down instead of egging him on. Do you have good friends in your life? Are you a good friend?

> When choosing friends, think quality over quantity. It's better to have one good friend than a dozen fake ones.

Let's talk about some of the things we can do to choose good friends. When choosing friends, think quality over quantity. It's better to have one good friend than a dozen fake ones.

The Bible provides tips on how to choose—and be—good friends. Much of the advice will be taken from the book of Proverbs[1]. We'll look at the principle behind each verse. And then, we'll examine a biblical example of true friendship.

The righteous choose their friends carefully, but the way of the wicked leads them astray (Proverbs 12:26 NIV).

It's important to choose your friends wisely. If you don't, you may be led down the wrong path. Do you have a friend who encourages you to do bad things? Or, have you witnessed someone who got caught up with the wrong crowd and got in trouble? The people we associate with have a lot of influence over us. They can impact the way we talk, dress, and act. They can even affect whether we drink alcohol or take drugs.

A friend is always loyal, and a brother is born to help in time of need (Proverbs 17:17 NLT).

A good friend always supports you. This does not mean they will allow you to do whatever you want. It means they want the best for you. Sometimes that might mean they have to get an adult involved in a situation when you feel they should have been excluded.

One who has unreliable friends soon comes to ruin, but there is a friend who sticks closer than a brother (Proverbs 18:24 NIV).

Reliability affects our friendships. Can your friends count on you? Do you have friends you can depend on? If you don't, Jesus is the Friend who sticks closer than a brother. He will never leave you or forsake you (Deuteronomy 31:6).

The New King James renders the first part of Proverbs 18:24 this way:

A man who has friends must himself be friendly

If we are going to have friends, we have to be friendly. We can't isolate ourselves and expect to attract people who want to be our friends. An expansion of this principle may be: if we want to have good friends, we must first be a good friend. In this way, we become the type of person we want to associate with.

Do not make friends with a hot-tempered person, do not associate with one easily angered, (Proverbs 22:24 NIV).

We have already seen in Haman's story how destructive anger can be. We don't want to be persons who give in to anger and hurts others. And we don't want friends like that either.

Love prospers when a fault is forgiven, but dwelling on it separates close friends (Proverbs 17:9 NLT).

The principle behind this proverb is forgiveness. How easily do you forgive the people who hurt you? The longer we dwell on our hurts, the more difficult it becomes to forgive.

An offended friend is harder to win back than a fortified city. Arguments separate friends like a gate locked with bars (Proverbs 18:19 NLT).

When we hurt the people we care about, it is sometimes difficult—or impossible—to restore the relationship. In a lot of ways, that's because of our ability to forgive. But it also reminds us to be careful of our actions. If we believe something we say or do will cause offense, it's better to avoid that action altogether. Words spoken cannot be recanted, and actions done cannot be undone.

Never abandon a friend—either yours or your father's. When disaster strikes, you won't have to ask your brother for assistance. It's better to go to a neighbor than to a brother who lives far away (Proverbs 27:10 NLT).

If you have a good friend, you should maintain that relationship. That means investing time and effort into your friendship. You can't say someone is your friend, but never talk to them or spend time with them. This also applies to our relationship with God. We have to nurture the bond so that it gets stronger over time.

Young people who obey the law are wise; those with wild friends bring shame to their parents (Proverbs 28:7 NLT).

I'm sure your parents have spoken to you about some of the people you associate with. That's because adults have a better instinct about people. It comes from years of observing others, as well as, their own experiences. It doesn't mean that we're always right, but if your parent, guardian, or another adult you trust warns you about a certain person, you may want to take heed. Find out what their concerns are, and then make your own observations. Please remember to pray and

111

ask God for wisdom. He knows everyone and He's never wrong.

It would be nice if you had a checklist you could use to evaluate a person to see if they were a good or bad friend. I won't create one for you because it's best if you come up with your own criteria.

Words spoken cannot be recanted, and actions done cannot be undone.

I hope after you have finished reading this chapter (and maybe do some research for yourself), you'll have a better idea of what a true friend looks like. Make your own checklist so that in the future you can refer to it if you're not sure whether someone is a good friend or not.

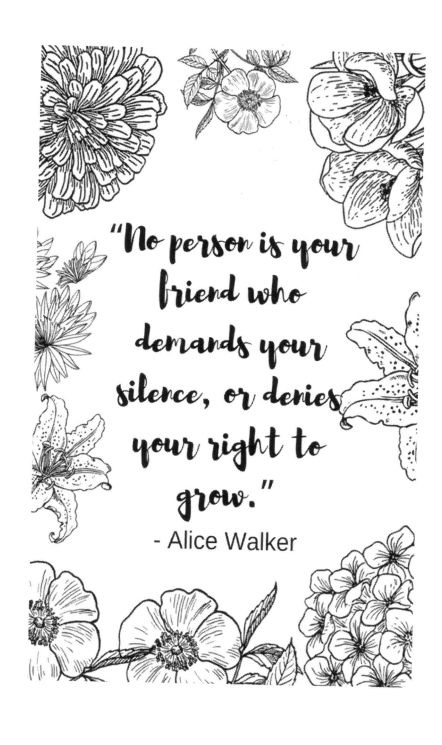

"No person is your friend who demands your silence, or denies your right to grow."

- Alice Walker

True friendship

So, I promised we'd talk about a biblical example of true friendship. In 1 Samuel 18:1–1 Samuel 20:41, we read the story of David and Jonathan (yeah, I know it's kind of long, but learning about the traits of a good friend is a long-term investment. Besides, you can always listen to it using an app like Bible Gateway or YouTube[2].)

At their first meeting, we are told that "the soul of Jonathan was knit to the soul of David" and that Jonathan loved David as "his own soul". But what is it that made Jonathan such a good friend to David? Here are five traits Jonathan had:

1. A good friend lets you know when somebody means you harm (1 Samuel 19:2).

Have you ever been in a situation where someone disliked you or said horrible things about you? How did you find out? Did you have a friend who told you what people were saying about you? Or what they were planning to do? Or, did you just wander blindly into whatever emotional trap was being set for you?

When Jonathan realized Saul wanted to kill David, he was upfront about it (I Samuel 19:2). That must have been one of the most awkward conversations in the history of awkward conversations:

"Ah, bro… you need to get away from here," says Jonathan.
"Um. No! I like it here. I'm in the army. The king let me marry his daughter…we started off a little sticky, but I think we're okay now." replies David. "Did I tell you I'm still on my honeymoon?"

"Eww, that's my sister. Well, anyway, my dad wants to kill you."
"Wait, what? I thought he was over that."
"Err, no."

2. Good friends speak well of you (I Samuel 19:4–5).

When I was younger I didn't have a lot of friends. As a person who spent a lot of time with my nose in a book, I wasn't such a popular choice when it came to playing games with the neighborhood kids. I didn't make myself friendly. I also knew enough to know the way they talked about me when they thought I wasn't there was a pretty, good indicator that they weren't fond of me.

A good friend—a really good one—speaks well of you even when you aren't there. They see all the good things about you. They recognize the things you're not so proud of and love you anyway. They see them as learning opportunities and give you grace—lots and lots of grace. They give you space to grow. A lot of time they are right there with you—struggling to get through the things you're struggling with because they care.

3. A true friend can be counted on (1 Samuel 20:4).

"A friend is someone who helps you up when you're down, and if they can't, they lay down beside you and listen[3]". David had such a friend in Jonathan. Even though the enemy was his own father, Jonathan was willing to stand in the gap between David and Saul.

4. A true pal is not envious of you (I Samuel 20:30).

I love watching teen movies. But I've noticed that there's a thread of envy which runs through a group of really popular girls. Typically, the leader keeps everyone in place by reminding them she is superior to them and they should be lucky she allows them to talk to her. Her popularity is maintained because of the envy everyone feels for her. Every girl wants to be her so they do anything to stay on her good side. This wasn't the case with Jonathan and David. As the son of the reigning king, Jonathan should have been next in line for the throne, but God had already chosen David as the next king.

Saul knew and so did Jonathan, yet he had no envy towards his friend. Like Saul, Jonathan should have plotted and schemed to have David killed. Instead, he wanted to preserve David's life knowing that it meant all the wealth and power of his father would never be his.

5. A friend mourns when you mourn (I Samuel 20:41).

There's nothing worse than going through heartache alone. As social beings, we handle situations better when we have someone there with us. A good friend is there not only when things are happy, but also when they are sad. Because they know and care about us, they are affected by the things that make us sad.

When David had to deal with the fact that he would have to leave his home, family, and friends, he was deeply distressed. So was Jonathan. Do you have a friend like that? Are you a friend like that to someone? There ought to be someone you can call on when things get a little rough. People need people.

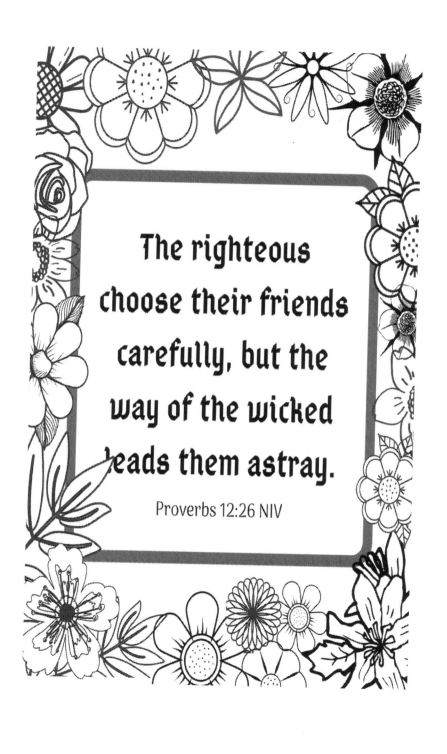

The righteous choose their friends carefully, but the way of the wicked leads them astray.

Proverbs 12:26 NIV

Now that we know what the qualities of a true friend are, here's one trait you don't need in a friend:

A good friend does not lead you into destruction. In Proverbs 1:10–19, we read:

My child, if sinners entice you,
turn your back on them!
They may say, "Come and join us.
Let's hide and kill someone!
Just for fun, let's ambush the innocent!
Let's swallow them alive, like the grave;
let's swallow them whole, like those who go down to the pit of death.
Think of the great things we'll get!
We'll fill our houses with all the stuff we take.
Come, throw in your lot with us;
we'll all share the loot."
My child, don't go along with them!
Stay far away from their paths.
They rush to commit evil deeds.
They hurry to commit murder.
If a bird sees a trap being set,
it knows to stay away.
But these people set an ambush for themselves;
they are trying to get themselves killed.
Such is the fate of all who are greedy for money;
it robs them of life (NLT).

So maybe the "bad friend" doesn't say, "Come let's go rob and kill." It could be as simple as, "Let's take something that doesn't belong to us." Or, "Let's say something is true when it isn't." We are told to stay far away from these people because they are headed for destruction and if we go along for the ride—we will be destroyed as well[4].

118

I hope this has given you some things to think about. I want you to spend a few minutes thinking about what makes a good friend, as well as, what makes a bad one. Go ahead and jot them down at the end of this chapter (if this is not your book, write your ideas in a journal).

Think about the people you have in your life. Do they have the traits of a good friend? (A good friend can sometimes do things which hurt us. It doesn't necessarily mean they are bad friends. It has everything to do with the intention behind the action. Before deciding someone is a bad friend, ask yourself "Why did [my friend] behave that way?")

Think about your actions up to this point: have you been a good friend? What can you do to become a better friend?

Make a good first impression

Queens-in-training need to understand the importance of making a good impression. You never get a second chance to make a first impression[5]. You never get a second chance to make a second, third or fiftieth impression. It's therefore important that we choose to make every impression count. Queen Esther knew this. And so, in chapter 5, she chose her clothing and her words wisely. Her every desire was to please the king. Her clothing, plan, mannerisms, and words were chosen with him in mind.

A good friend...

....

....

....

....

....

....

....

....

....

A bad friend...

In every situation, we ought to be thinking of how we can be ambassadors of our Heavenly Father. Here are some things we can ask ourselves:

- Would my words please God?
- Is my outfit modest and befitting of a queen-to-be?
- Does my body language project a positive image?
- Does my facial expression tell a story consistent with my words?
- Am I speaking and acting in a manner that others would want to emulate?

If your answer to any of the questions above is no, it means you need to readjust. Before you tell me how difficult it is to do these things, let me share some things you would have to change if you were a princess of an earthly monarchy.

Social media—members of the royal family are not allowed to maintain an individual social media account. Rather, there's an official one for the Royal Family that is maintained by professionals.

Your personal style—princesses must be impeccably groomed and modestly dressed at all times. They have royal dressers who choose their clothing according to the standard set by the monarch.

Privacy—your life will constantly be under scrutiny by every member of your country and the rest of the world.

The freedom to go to the store by yourself—for security reasons, you are not allowed to go out in public without protection. And while that might seem like a cool thing, it means every purchase you make will be witnessed (and possibly reported) by your security detail.

Selfies—well, I guess you can still take these if you're by yourself (but then again, where would you post it since your personal social media accounts are closed and it can't go on the royal feed).

A career—being a royal is a full-time job so any dream you had of becoming anything other than a princess would have to be put aside.

Voting rights—you are not allowed to vote as doing so would compromise your impartiality. This also means you would have to keep your political opinions to yourself[6].

Many of us think the idea of marrying a prince is like being in a fairytale. Maybe you even daydream about it happening to you. Would you be willing to do these things if it meant you'd be a princess? Then why is it so hard to do them to become a queen in a heavenly kingdom?

As queens-in-training, we learn to represent our king in everything we say and do. It doesn't mean we never make mistakes. It means when we do, we apologize where possible, seek forgiveness and move on. We'll have other opportunities to serve our Heavenly Master and we won't be able to do that if we're wallowing in mistakes of the past.

8

Don't Be Ruled By Anger

The world teaches us we should have everything we want and do whatever we want to do. It gives the impression that we are able to act without following rules without repercussion. But that's not the truth. A person who does what he wants at all times will eventually start to believe they can take what they want without consequences. The same society that tells us it's okay to do what we want, calls it stealing when we do. Theft breaks the laws of the land and those who break the law will be penalized.

What are you angry about?

In Esther 3, we met Haman—a prince who had been elevated over all the others because the king favored him. There is no record that he had done anything to warrant this favor, but we have already seen that King Xerxes is a man who does as he pleases regardless of the consequences. Haman seems to have been a proud man who thought overmuch of himself. He reveled in the seeming adoration of the people. Did he know they were only showing him reverence because the king demanded it? Undoubtedly, but he didn't seem to care.

I imagine him preening as he walked among the people who fell down before him. He didn't notice the one man who did not bow. He was the prime minister and didn't need to pay attention to the common people.

But when it was reported to him that Mordecai did not kneel or bow down when he passed, he took notice. He looked at every man to confirm that they were giving him the proper respect. Oh, how it burned him when he realized there was one man who dared to look him in the eye when he passed. The Bible tells us he was enraged (Esther 3:5).

Let us look a little at the original Hebrew word translated as enraged. The word is chêmâh (pronounced khay-maw') meaning heat; figuratively, anger, poison (from its fever), anger, hot displeasure, furious, heat, indignation, poison, rage, wrath, wrathful[1].

Have you ever been so angry you felt as if you were burning? Or, as if the top of your head was going to blow off? That's the kind of anger Haman felt. How dare Mordecai not kneel when he passed? How dare the Jews disobey the king's command to worship him?

In his anger, Haman forgot about all the thousands—probably hundreds of thousands or even millions—who bowed before him and instead focused on one man. He decided that it was not enough to destroy Mordecai—the man who would not kneel—he had to destroy all of Mordecai's people.

This kind of anger is dangerous because it leads to generalization. We do this sometimes. We are attacked by a dog so we hate all dogs. We have difficulty with our Math teacher, so we believe all Math teachers are evil. Or, that Math is difficult and unnecessary. The Bible tells us "be angry but do not sin" (Ephesians 4:26). I like the way the New Living Translation renders that verse:

And "don't sin by letting anger control you." Don't let the sun go down while you are still angry,

Is God telling us we should not get angry? No, anger is a natural human emotion, one we received from Him. But we should not allow our anger to cause us to do things which hurt others or ourselves.

Haman's anger was destructive. It burned out of control and would not be sated until he had murdered every Jew in the 127 provinces of Media and Persia. He was even willing to pay the equivalent of over three million pounds[2] to destroy the Jews. Historians estimate that during the reign of King Darius, Xerxes' father, the taxes from the empire resulted in an annual income of 10 000 talents[3]. That's a lot of money!

Has that happened to you? Have you ever been so angry you wanted to destroy something or harm someone? Each of us has or will experience the irrational behavior that comes from unadulterated rage. It may be hard for you to comprehend but you are a queen-in-training. We must remember Christ gives us the strength to do things which would otherwise be impossible (Philippians 4:13).

Effects of anger

Hurtful words—when people are angry they say mean things. Sometimes the things we say in our anger are true but should have been said in a kinder, more loving way. Other times, we say things we know will hurt the person we're angry at. Words spoken cannot be recalled. And though we may apologize, we can never fully undo the impact or the memory of words spoken in anger.

Anger can destroy relationships which cannot be repaired.

Rash actions—anger can cause us to do things we later regret. Like words, our actions cannot be undone and the impacts linger for a long time. Anger can lead to uncharacteristic behavior which leaves a lasting impression in the mind of the person who witnesses it.

I'm sure you've experienced the devastation of unrestrained anger. Try to remember how you felt when you were the recipient of someone's unchecked anger. It's easy to give vent to our anger but the damage caused can take months—or years—to repair. In fact, anger can destroy relationships beyond repair.

Why we should not get angry

As queens-in-training, we are hoping to one day receive a reward when Jesus returns. The reward is a mansion in heaven and the chance to reign with God. But we can only receive this reward if we are clothed in the righteousness of God. Only people who are righteous can stand in God's presence. Anger does not produce the kind of righteousness God desires (James 1:19–20).

Anger causes strife. A queen is called to quiet contention and promote peace (Proverbs 15:18). How can we create a desire for peace in others if we are the ones stirring up anger?

Anger leads to acts of vengeance. The Bible teaches that vengeance belongs to the Lord (Romans 12:19). When we're angry, we believe we have to defend ourselves. In most cases, we hurt persons around us. Allow God to avenge you. I promise you He will in the proper time and when He does, there will be no repercussions or backlash for you.

Why we should control our anger

There is one major reason we should control our tempers: we are called to emulate God. What does that mean? We are created in the image and likeness of God which means we have similar characteristics and traits. Does that mean God gets angry? Yes, it does. But His anger is not like ours.

God gets angry sometimes but it is righteous anger. This type of anger is out of the realm for humanity because only God knows everything and the intent behind every action. As they say, there are three sides to every story: mine, yours and the truth. Simply put, each person will have their version of the story. This will be filtered through their thoughts, expectations, desires, history, and understanding of the situation and the other person's motive.

There will be a version with just facts. The truth. Only God can truly understand what each person was thinking, feeling or hoping to accomplish. That's why He's the only Person capable of being a judge. And the thing of it is, even though God knows, sees and understands everything, He's slow to anger. Can you imagine if God got angry as quickly and easily as some of us do?

There would probably be no earth left and certainly, there would be no one on the planet. The Holy Spirit wants to teach us godly anger—the kind that's slow-burning and not quick to rash actions or decisions. God is slow to anger (Psalm 103:8) and we should be the same.

Tips for controlling our anger

Focus on who we represent—We are ambassadors of the Great King. By focusing on who we represent—God—we remember to control our actions because what we do tells others about Him. Would you want to be represented by a foul-mouthed, angry person who fought everyone who got in their way? While this may not an exact representation of you angry, it's a good image to keep in mind because God doesn't want to be represented by anyone who does not share His character.

A good queen is wise. Sometimes that means not saying everything that comes into our thoughts. Anger removes the filter between our brains and mouths. It's best to keep quiet until our temper is abated.

Create a process for managing your anger—Spend some time trying to figure out the best way to calm yourself after you have gotten angry. Do you need some time alone? Do you listen to music? Read? Write letters? Whatever it is, create a process and rehearse it. You may think my advice is contradictory: first I tell you not to get angry, and then I tell you to practice being angry. Allow me to explain: did you know the reason most people panic in an emergency is because they don't know what to do?

That's why companies plan and practice fire drills. Organizations and some homes have a fire plan[4] which includes regular fire drills. Members of staff are informed of the evacuation process and told where they should evacuate to in the event of an emergency. They simulate the evacuation process through fire drills. By practicing what to do when there is no emergency, they increase the likelihood that people will know what to do when there is an emergency.

This is what I mean when I talk about a process. Decide what you're going to do when you get angry. Write it down if you have to and then practice it until it becomes your default reaction when you are angry. When I was much younger I would give vent to my anger. I would say whatever came to my mind. But after observing the effects of my anger on the people around me, I wanted to become a different person. I started practicing holding my peace when I got angry.

My anger cooldown process

....

....

....

....

....

....

....

....

It became so much of a habit that I am now able to keep my anger inside while treating the person I'm angry with in a respectful manner. Think of it as being a good customer relations manager. You are not only representing God, you are also representing yourself. How do you want people to perceive you? The way we behave has a lot to do with what people think of us.

The art of forgiveness

The story of Haman and Mordecai is one about forgiveness. In Haman's mind, Mordecai had wronged him by not treating him with the respect that came with his office. Haman had to make a choice: did he forgive Mordecai, or hold a grudge?

Haman nursed his angry feelings towards Mordecai. He built it up until the only thing which could satisfy him was Mordecai's death. And the destruction of everyone even remotely connected to Mordecai.

It's easy for us to say "forgive and forget" but forgiveness is not always easy. Especially when the person who offended us doesn't apologize. So, how do you get over what they did to you so you can forgive them when they won't even say they're sorry?

It helps if we think of forgiveness as an action and a process. It takes work and a lot of effort on our part to stop feeling angry or resentful towards someone for something they did. It takes practice for us to not think about how we wish they would suffer or be repaid for what they've done to us. But it's something we need to do.

Let's talk about why we need to forgive. When we're angry, our heart rate and blood pressure increases. This can, in turn, increase our risk of diseases such as heart attacks, strokes, or depression[5]. Unforgiveness can affect our ability to sleep and make it difficult for us to concentrate[6].

Along with the physical effects of anger and unforgiveness, there are also spiritual implications. This is what the Bible has to say:

For all have sinned and fall short of the glory of God, (Romans 3:23 ESV).

Be kind to one another, tenderhearted, forgiving one another, as God in Christ forgave you (Ephesians 4:32 ESV).

For if you forgive others their trespasses, your heavenly Father will also forgive you, but if you do not forgive others their trespasses, neither will your Father forgive your trespasses (Matthew 6:14–15 ESV).

Then Peter came up and said to him, "Lord, how often will my brother sin against me, and I forgive him? As many as seven times?" Jesus said to him, "I do not say to you seven times, but seventy times seven (Matthew 18:21–22 ESV).

As queens-in-training, we have to understand that every one of us has sinned against God. Because of sin, all we deserve is death (Romans 6:23). But God didn't give us what we deserved. Instead, He sent His Son who paid the price of sin on our behalf. Jesus died a horrible, painful death so that we could be forgiven. God expects us to forgive each other because He forgave us. If we don't, we will not be forgiven for our sins.

So, how do we begin the process of forgiveness? The first step may be to accept that the person who wronged us may never apologize. They may not even realize they had offended us. We have to admit our feelings of hurt, anger or whatever else may be rolling around in our heads and hearts. We're facing our feelings—not to dwell on them—but to examine them so we can release them.

Talk about your feelings. Do you have someone you trust with whom you can discuss what happened and how you're feeling about it? Make some time to talk with that person. But know if there's no one you can talk to on earth, our Heavenly Father is always willing to listen to us.

Another good way to process your emotion is to speak with the person who wronged you. Do not approach them when you are still angry. When you are calm, talk to them about what happened and how you felt about it. This may not always be possible depending on the situation. An alternative is to write them a letter which expresses how you feel. Once you are through, destroy the letter.

As you work through the forgiveness process, pray about it. Ask God to help you forgive the person and move past what they have done. Ask Him to reveal if there is a lesson He wants you to learn. Pray for the person.

Ask God to be with them and fill them with the Holy Spirit so they can be transformed into His likeness. Now, I know, praying for someone who hurt you is the last thing you want to do. Jesus knew it too, which is why He said:

"You have heard that it was said, 'Love your neighbor and hate your enemy.' But I tell you, love your enemies and pray for those who persecute you, that you may be children of your Father in heaven. He causes his sun to rise on the evil and the good, and

I need to forgive...

···

···

···

These are the steps I'll take...

···

···

···

···

···

···

sends rain on the righteous and the unrighteous" (Matthew 5:43–45 NIV).

As we pray for the people who hurt us, we draw closer to God and become more like Him and that's ultimately what we want.

Handling Conflict

Diplomacy and finesse are two skills needed for queens-in-training. In case you're wondering what I mean, let me explain what I mean by diplomacy and finesse. Diplomacy is the ability, or skill of managing our relationships with others, whereas finesse is the knack of dealing with things tactfully and discretely. As ambassadors of the Great King, these are skills we need to refine. When we handle things poorly, it puts us—and our Heavenly Father—in a bad light.

One of the major themes of Esther is the way people react when they are challenged. Haman's response was to request and arrange the slaughter of all the people who shared the religion of his enemy. His decision was supported by his friends and family.

Haman's friends and his wife advised him to erect a gallows and ask the king permission to have Mordecai hanged on it (Esther 5:14). He wanted the gallows to be exceptionally high so that it could be seen by people from miles away[7].

At that time in Persia, only the king could approve a man's death. Otherwise, I'm sure Haman would have found some way to have Mordecai killed immediately. It wasn't enough that the extermination of Mordecai and his people was a few short months away. Haman wanted to expedite the death of the one whom he considered his personal nemesis.

What would Haman have done had he been able to put himself in Mordecai's shoes? Is it possible he could have found a way to face his enemy without murdering an entire nationality? This encounter could have been handled well if he had employed a little tact and may have been avoided altogether if he had thought about it.

Mordecai hadn't actually done anything to him. He had simply refused to bow. Haman's problem was that he had begun to believe the deference requested by the king was his due and right.

How do we respond to our enemies?

We are not going to be liked by everyone. No matter how nice you are or how well you behave there will be persons who dislike you. Their reasons will vary and may not always make sense to you. So the sooner you get used to that idea, the better off you'll be. Put it this way: no matter how pretty your pictures are on social media or how entertaining your captions, some people will dislike your posts and others will unfriend you. The real dilemma is how will you respond to it?

Esther and Haman responded to their enemies in different ways. Yes, I know, it seems unbelievable that Haman would consider Mordecai his enemy when they had had no conversation. But, as I said, enmity can form in different ways. Let's dig into the two responses.

Haman's response

When Haman saw that Mordecai would not bow down or show him respect, he was filled with rage. He had learned of Mordecai's nationality, so he decided it was not enough to lay hands on Mordecai alone. Instead, he looked for a way to destroy all the Jews throughout the entire empire of Xerxes (Esther 3:5-6 NLT).

Haman's response to Mordecai's refusal to bow down went through a few phases:

1. He assumed it had to do with a lack of respect.
2. He became angry.
3. He investigated Mordecai's background (or maybe he just took note of what the person said when they explained why Mordecai said he would not bow.)
4. He decided it wasn't enough to destroy Mordecai alone. He would destroy all of Mordecai's people as well.
5. He made a plan to annihilate the Jews. But first, he chose the perfect day by casting lots (that would be almost like consulting a fortune teller or psychic).
6. He approached the king with bribery and sly words.
7. He dictated a decree that all Jews—regardless of age or gender—must be killed.

The only person who had disrespected Haman (in his eyes) was Mordecai. A better response would have been for him to approach Mordecai and ask him to explain why he would not bow. Had Haman done so, he would have known Mordecai's reason for not bowing down. He would have learned a bit more about the Jewish culture and may even have gotten a better appreciation for its people.

Instead, we see a man who only cared about his needs and desires. He allowed his anger to drive his decision-making and in the end sealed his own fate.

Esther's response

When Esther learned that her people would be killed at Haman's request, her first response was fear (more on this later). But, once she decided to intervene, she took the following steps:

1. She asked Mordecai to fast on her behalf. He was also instructed to invite the Jews in Susa to fast as well.

2. She and her maids fasted.

3. She made a plan to approach the king and made preparations to execute it.

4. She dressed with deliberation.

5. She humbled herself before the king.

6. She did not blurt out her request. She ensured that the setting was right before she asked for what she wanted.

Was Esther angry when she heard that her people were about to be killed? Maybe. I think she would also have been scared. Because even if she escaped the genocide[8] planned for her people, her cousin Mordecai wouldn't. Neither would her former neighbors nor any of the people she remembered from her life as Mordecai's adopted daughter. This would have left her feeling emotional and decisions made in an emotional state are not always the best ones.

Esther gave herself a three-day timeout. During this time she would get her emotions under control and make plans. She would figure out the best way to approach the king and she'd rehearse.

Have you ever been in a situation where someone said something to which you wanted to respond but the words wouldn't come? And then, two days later you think of the perfect response. Well, this wouldn't happen to Esther because she was not reacting while she was processing her emotions.

Another reason Esther chose not to approach the king immediately was that she knew the matter was too big for her to handle on her own. How would she, a woman whom Xerxes had not wanted to see for one month, be able to influence him to spare her life? How would she ask him to spare her people? How would she influence him to choose her over his favorite courtier whom he probably saw every day? She wasn't. Not unless she first sought God's favor and it was His desire.

My dear queen-in-training, you are going to face many things in your life—some will seem easy while others, impossible. However, regardless of how you judge your ability to accomplish it on your own, know that it is God who makes things happen.

You can make many plans, but the LORD's purpose will prevail (Proverbs 19:21 NLT).

So whether you believe you can do it in your own strength or not, learn from Esther and lean into your Heavenly Father. Whenever you face a decision here are some interesting verses to meditate on:

Trust in the Lord with all your heart, and do not lean on your own understanding. In all your ways acknowledge him, and he will make straight your paths (Proverbs 3:5–6 ESV).

And my God shall supply all your need according to His riches in glory by Christ Jesus (Philippians 4:19 NKJV).

Seek the Lord and his strength; seek his presence continually! (1 Chronicles 16:11 ESV).

I can do all things through Christ who strengthens me (Philippians 4:13 NKJV).

Fear not, for I am with you; be not dismayed, for I am your God; I will strengthen you, I will help you, I will uphold you with my righteous right hand (Isaiah 41:10 ESV).

"For with God, nothing will be impossible" (Luke 1:37 NKJV).

9

Is Fear a Strength or a Weakness?

*E*sther 5 begins three days after Esther's fast. She was ready to face the king. I can imagine that after three days with nothing to eat or drink, the thing foremost on her mind was food. But she put away her sackcloth and ashes and dressed in her queen's finery. I want you to picture her with me:

She took a perfumed bath and massaged her skin with the best Persian beauty treatments available. She asked one of her maids to bring her most beautiful gown. Maybe she wore the dress in which she first met the king. Or, she chose a dress which accentuated her best features.

Once she was dressed, she took a deep breath and opened the door to her room. She was going to see the king.

Make plans

The Bible doesn't say much except that she put on her royal robes (Esther 5:1). But there was something significant about those words. It signaled a woman who fully embraced her role as queen—maybe for the first time since she had been crowned. It showed a woman ready to stand between her people and the man who wanted to destroy them. It showed a woman who acknowledged that it was time to do the right thing and was willing to lose her life in the process. It also showed a woman with a plan.

The Persian throne room was arranged so the king sat facing the courtyard. Because she knew the rule, Queen Esther stood in the courtyard until acknowledged. The king was pleased with her and held out the golden scepter. Please note this did not happen by chance. Remember we talked about God's Providence? This is Providence at work again. The queen approached the king and touched the tip of the scepter. By doing that she communicated her willingness to submit to his authority[1].

Notice what happened next: the king asked her what she wanted. She didn't blurt it out in a room which was no doubt filled with the king's princes and courtiers. She didn't fumble and try to come up with a plan on spot. She invited the king and Haman to a banquet she had prepared. This shows advance planning. The banquet as ready; all that was mi.. were the guests of honor. This did a number of things:

1. It showed the king she had thought about him. She didn't invite him for a meal and then have him wait hours for it to be prepared. It was available before she made her request so he and Haman could immediately attend the banquet.

2. She isolated the two persons most impacted by her request. By removing the king and Haman from the throne room, she had the chance for a more intimate conversation. She also removed the king from the influence of the advisors who would seek to twist Esther's request and put her in a bad light.

She also separated Haman from his supporters and those who would vouch or beg for him. Remember, the Persian men remained separate from the women so Esther would find no support in a room full of men. It's possible many of them would have been seeing her for the first time. And even if they had seen her before, they had had no opportunity to develop a relationship with her. As such, they would have had no reason to support her request in front of the king.

3. She showed the king she knew enough about him to know who his favorite courtier was. The king had no idea Haman had been identified as an enemy of the Jews. He only knew his queen had invited him and his favorite prince to a banquet she had prepared.

A word on Persian eating practices before we move on. The Persian meal had two courses: the first consisted of meats and other staples. They drank only water with this meal. The second course consisted of fruits and wine[2]. Ordinarily, the king and queen dined separately, each in their own rooms. The king occasionally invited his courtiers to join him for the second course[3]. An invitation to eat with both the king and queen was a sign that you were favored. No wonder Haman was ecstatic.

At the banquet of wine, the king renewed his request to grant Esther anything her heart desired even if it was half his kingdom (Esther 5:6). What would you have done? Many of us would have blurted out our request at that time, and maybe it would have been granted. But sometimes it's best to wait so that we can evaluate and make the best plans.

I believe Esther didn't tell Xerxes what she wanted initially because of her fast. I think she had asked God for the king to be willing to attend a second banquet as a sign she had received God's favor. Or maybe it had everything to do with God's perfect timing.

Not stating her request immediately also served to build anticipation. The king left his queen's presence wondering what she wanted of him. Haman left with the impression that he was an important man who had the favor of both the king and queen.

The banquet was a turning point for Haman. He had been honored so he had an opportunity to honor another person. On his way home, he saw Mordecai the Jew—the man whose people he had sworn to destroy. A compassionate man would have looked at Mordecai and thought about all

148

the things he had received and want to bless him as he had been blessed. But as we see in Esther 5:9, that was not the case. When Haman saw Mordecai he was filled with rage.

Haman went out that day happy and in high spirits. But when he saw Mordecai at the king's gate and observed that he neither rose nor showed fear in his presence, he was filled with rage against Mordecai. Nevertheless, Haman restrained himself and went home.
Calling together his friends and Zeresh, his wife, Haman boasted to them about his vast wealth, his many sons, and all the ways the king had honored him and how he had elevated him above the other nobles and officials. "And that's not all," Haman added. "I'm the only person Queen Esther invited to accompany the king to the banquet she gave. And she has invited me along with the king tomorrow. But all this gives me no satisfaction as long as I see that Jew Mordecai sitting at the king's gate" (Esther 5:9–13 NIV).

Maybe you're wondering what's happening here. Why would Haman need to tell his friends and his wife all that he had? Didn't they already know? In Persia, a man proved himself by his skill in battle and the number of sons he had[4]. Basically, Haman told his friends that all the things he had meant nothing to him as long as Mordecai was alive.

Can you imagine hating someone that much? Let me take a moment to say something you may have heard before: hate hurts you more than the person it is directed at. Half the time the person you hate doesn't realize how you feel about them. And if they do, they don't care (at least, not as much as you do).

Put yourself in Esther's position for a few minutes. Your beloved cousin—the one who raised you after your parents' death—had told you that in a few months he and everyone

ı knew would be killed. For no reason at all. You had
.een living in the castle for a few years and though you hadn't
told anyone your religion, it's possible that people knew, or
suspected. Your life was quite literally in danger. What would
you do? How would you feel?

I'd be scared with a touch of paranoia. I'd start
wondering who knew my background. I'd view everyone's
actions with suspicion. I'd wonder which one of them wanted
to start the slaughter early and suspect everyone of trying to
kill me. When Mordecai first informed Esther that the lives of
her people were at stake, he expected her to rush into the
king's courtyard and beg for them. This would have come as
a huge surprise to the king who had no idea she was Jewish.

"All the king's officials and the people of the royal provinces
know that for any man or woman who approaches the king in the
inner court without being summoned the king has but one law: that
they be put to death unless the king extends the gold scepter to
them and spares their lives. But thirty days have passed since I was
called to go to the king" (Esther 4:11 NLT).

Using our fear for good

Xerxes may have chosen her because he favored her
more than all the other virgins, but it had been thirty days
since he had asked to see her. Esther was no longer sure of
her place in his affections. She didn't want to do anything to
displease him because that could result in her death. It
seemed as though death was on every side for this young

queen. What was she going to do? If she spoke up, she could die. If she didn't speak up, she could die.

Mordecai's response could have seemed unnecessarily harsh to young Esther or could have been taken as a source of inspiration.

"Do not think that because you are in the king's house you alone of all the Jews will escape. For if you remain silent at this time, relief and deliverance for the Jews will arise from another place, but you and your father's family will perish. And who knows but that you have come to your royal position for such a time as this?" (Esther 4:13–14 NLT).

We know she took his words as inspiration because of what she did next. But can you imagine how she felt as she made her decision? It would have been an agonizing decision

A truly brave person is one who feels fear and does what needs to be done in spite of their fear.

to make. Sometimes fear can paralyze us, preventing us from doing what needs to be done. Esther was able to tap into her fear and use it to channel her in the right direction.

This is a lesson we all need to learn. We think people are brave because they don't feel fear. But a truly brave person is one who feels fear and does what needs to be done in spite of their fear. This is not permission to do something foolish or dangerous. Quite the contrary, it's an invitation to do those things which cause you to grow and thrive in your roles here on earth as you prepare to live and reign in heaven.

When God created the world, there was no fear. But sin brought with it many things, one of those being the fear which so many of us experience daily. There are many things to fear, things like:

- Fitting in with our peers
- Missing out on things
- Being inadequate or failing
- Insects and animals

There's an infinite list of things to fear and a phobia for everything you can think of. It may seem easier to avoid the things which scare us, but here's a funny thing about fear: it doesn't stay contained. If you allow it to dominate one area of your life, it will soon start to affect other areas until you become so fearful it's difficult for you to do a lot of things.

If fear is so crippling, how do we get past it in order to do what we have to do? Here are a couple of steps to follow the next time something scares you:

1. Remember that fear does not come from God.

For God has not given us a spirit of fear, but of power and of love and of a sound mind. (2 Timothy 1:7 NKJV).

152

2. We can do everything through Christ—even the things that scare us.

I can do all things through Christ who strengthens me (Philippians 4:13 NKJV).

3. Fear gives us an opportunity to lean on God whose strength becomes stronger in our weakness.

But he said to me, "My grace is sufficient for you, for my power is made perfect in weakness." Therefore I will boast all the more gladly about my weaknesses, so that Christ's power may rest on me (2 Corinthians 12:9 NIV).

4. Find role models. Since there's nothing new under the sun, the thing which scares you (or something like it) has been experienced by someone else. Tell yourself that if they can overcome their fear, so can you. If they can accomplish a particular task, then so can you.

5. Make a list of Bible verses and promises that will encourage you when you are feeling fearful. There's something soothing about the word of God. When we meditate on what God says, our focus becomes fixed on Him and away from the thing which scares us.

6. Rehearse facing your fears. Yup, I say that a lot. But one of the reasons we're afraid is because we don't know what to expect. Or, maybe we don't have any experience with thing that scares us. So if you're afraid of speaking in front of your peers, practice it. Practice reading aloud until you're

comfortable doing it. Then, read for one person like your mom or best friend. Keep increasing the audience as you become more comfortable.

If you still need more help on how to face your fears, you may find this series of blog posts helpful: https://bit.ly/FacingOurFears.

As queen-in-training, we have to work on the things that scare us because we can't allow fear to prevent us from doing the things God will ask us to do. In fact, it's been my experience that when God gives you an assignment, it will be bigger than anything you can accomplish on your own. Fear is a normal response but it shouldn't end there. As we work through our fear, we get an opportunity to partner with God to undertake the assignments He has given us.

My fear-fighting process

My fear-fighting Bible promises

....

....

....

....

....

....

....

....

....

My Attitude Towards God

The time you spend alone with God will transform your character and increase your devotion. Then your integrity and godly behavior in an unbelieving world will make others long to know the Lord.

— Charles Stanley

10

Preparing for Spiritual Warfare

*O*n the surface, the book of Esther is about a man who believed he wasn't getting the respect he deserved and sought to destroy all traces of the people he believed had snubbed him. We can even say it was about a man who sought to destroy his enemies—the Jewish people. Both perspectives are correct, but there's a deeper story here. It started in the Garden of Eden near the beginning of time.

The history of the world

You may already be familiar with the story. In the beginning, God created the heavens and the earth (Genesis 1:1). God made a perfect earth which He filled with plants, animals and two perfect people. Adam and Eve were given the freedom to do what they wanted. There was only one stated rule. They could eat freely of all the trees of the garden except for the Tree of the Knowledge of Good and Evil. "Because," God warned them, "the day you eat it you shall surely die" (Genesis 2:16–17).

Unfortunately, our fore parents didn't listen and sin entered the world. Before we talk about the over-arching story, let me pre-empt some questions you may have: why did God create people if He knew they would disobey Him? Why did God create the Tree of Knowledge in the first place? Why did He give Adam and Eve free will?

First things first, after God created humanity; there was a war in heaven. Was this a physical war? It's doubtful. The Bible, for the most part, explains things in ways we can understand and relate to. The beings in heaven are spiritual beings so this was more of a spiritual war than a physical one. I like to think of it as a legal debate, or a war of words.

At that time, Lucifer was one of the chief covering angels—he was pretty high up the chain of command. Put it this way: if God is king, he was the Prime Minister. If God is President, Lucifer was vice-president or at least a member of parliament. Jesus was the Son of God and equal with Him.

"You were the model of perfection,
    full of wisdom and exquisite in beauty.

You were in Eden,
> the garden of God.

Your clothing was adorned with every precious stone—
> red carnelian, pale-green peridot, white moonstone,
> blue-green beryl, onyx, green jasper,
> blue lapis lazuli, turquoise, and emerald—

all beautifully crafted for you
> and set in the finest gold.

They were given to you
> on the day you were created.

I ordained and anointed you
> as the mighty angelic guardian.

You had access to the holy mountain of God
> and walked among the stones of fire.

"You were blameless in all you did
> from the day you were created
> until the day evil was found in you.

Your rich commerce led you to violence,
> and you sinned.

So I banished you in disgrace
> from the mountain of God.

I expelled you, O mighty guardian,
> from your place among the stones of fire.

Your heart was filled with pride
> because of all your beauty.

Your wisdom was corrupted
> by your love of splendor.

So I threw you to the ground
> and exposed you to the curious gaze of kings"

(Ezekiel 28:12–17 NLT).

If you read all of Ezekiel 28, you'll realize that it was addressed to the King of Tyre. It may confuse you when you read about him being in the Garden of Eden. That's because the Bible often has parallel stories happening at the same time (call it the A story and the B story). We have to look at the clues in Scripture and use other parts of the Bible to help us understand what's happening.

Though it's addressed to the King of Tyre, it's also talking about Lucifer (or Satan as he's sometimes called). It was Lucifer who became filled with pride and became corrupted. Like us, the angels have free will. He insinuated that God was less than fair. He managed to convince one-third of the angels that he was right. He and his followers were thrown to the earth and the problems for humanity began.

And war broke out in heaven: Michael and his angels fought with the dragon; and the dragon and his angels fought, but they did not prevail, nor was a place found for them in heaven any longer. So the great dragon was cast out, that serpent of old, called the Devil and Satan, who deceives the whole world; he was cast to the earth, and his angels were cast out with him.

Then I heard a loud voice saying in heaven, "Now salvation, and strength, and the kingdom of our God, and the power of His Christ have come, for the accuser of our brethren, who accused them before our God day and night, has been cast down. And they overcame him by the blood of the Lamb and by the word of their testimony, and they did not love their lives to the death. Therefore rejoice, O heavens, and you who dwell in them! Woe to the inhabitants of the earth and the sea! For the devil has come down to you, having great wrath, because he knows that he has a short time" (Revelation 12:7–12 NLT).

In the Garden, Lucifer employed the same tactics he had used in heaven: wordplay. He convinced Eve to disobey God.

Now the serpent was more cunning than any beast of the field which the Lord God had made. And he said to the woman, "Has God indeed said, 'You shall not eat of every tree of the garden'?"

And the woman said to the serpent, "We may eat the fruit of the trees of the garden; but of the fruit of the tree which is in the midst of the garden, God has said, 'You shall not eat it, nor shall you touch it, lest you die.'"

Then the serpent said to the woman, "You will not surely die. For God knows that in the day you eat of it your eyes will be opened, and you will be like God, knowing good and evil".

So when the woman saw that the tree was good for food, that it was pleasant to the eyes, and a tree desirable to make one wise, she took of its fruit and ate. She also gave to her husband with her, and he ate. Then the eyes of both of them were opened, and they knew that they were naked; and they sewed fig leaves together and made themselves coverings (Genesis 3:1–7 NKJV).

Now that we have the history out of the way, let's start answering questions.

Why did God create people if He knew they would disobey Him?

The world and all the things in it were created out of an overflow of God's love. We were created to give honor and glory to God.

"'Bring all who claim me as their God, for I have made them for my glory. It was I who created them'" (Isaiah 43:7 NLT).

God knew we would sin but He loved us too much not to give us the chance to choose to love Him back. Think of it this way: children do things that are not nice or which make parents unhappy. However, most parents would still choose to have the children they have in spite of what they know about them (they may want to change the circumstances in which the child was born, but not the child themselves).

> *Regardless of your relationship with your parents or the circumstances of your birth, God loves you.*

Thinking of it that way gives us an inkling of how God feels about us—how He feels about you. Regardless of your relationship with your parents or the circumstances of your birth, God loves you. He chose to give you life and have you born at the time you were. God has a plan for your life and His plan and timing are perfect.

Why did He give mankind free will?

Free will is about choice. We have to freedom to choose to love or hate, obey or disobey. God created us because He loved us and He had this huge reserve of love that He wanted to share. He wants us to love Him too. He wants us to obey, serve, and love Him because we choose to—not because we are forced. Without the freedom to choose, we would be automatons or robots with no true emotion. God doesn't want that.

Think of it this way: you get to choose how you feel about every person you come in contact with, whether in person or through another medium. You decide if you love, like or hate them. Oh, they influence us by their actions and words, but we choose how we respond to their behavior.

Why did God create the Tree of Knowledge in the first place?

The Tree of the Knowledge of Good and Evil was part of mankind's ability to choose. God gave them an instruction:

"You can eat as much as you want of the other trees except this one."

He also gave them the consequence for disobedience:

"The day you eat of the Tree of Knowledge you shall surely die."

The Bible doesn't tell us if God explained all the steps that would have to happen before they died. Or, even if He explained what death meant. But, they had a choice. Before you start getting mad at God, think about your own life. You have been given a lot of instructions in your lifetime. Sometimes you are told what the consequence for disobedience will be and sometimes you're not. But are you always told *why* you should obey?

I'm guessing your answer is no, at least, that has been my experience. I've also realized that sometimes if I wait long enough, the answer either becomes clear or is explained to me. The Tree of Knowledge was a test of Adam and Eve's willingness to obey God. They could choose to focus on all the things they could eat, or on the one thing they couldn't have.

PAUSE TO PONDER

How often do I focus on things I can't have?

Okay, so now that we have all the questions out of the way, let's get back to the point of this chapter: what was the underlying story for the near-annihilation of the Jews?

Spiritual warfare

After Lucifer deceived Eve (spoiler alert: Lucifer was the snake), God made him a promise:

"And I will put enmity between you and the woman, and between your offspring and hers; he will crush your head, and you will strike his heel" (Genesis 3:15 NIV).

This was the first time in Scripture that God had promised the redemption of humanity. Basically, He told Lucifer that he and the human race would always be enemies. And someday there was going to be an epic battle. Lucifer would strike the heel of the offspring who would come from the woman, but his head would be crushed. He (Lucifer) would be defeated.

Even though Lucifer tried to get the woman to think God had told a lie about the Tree of Knowledge, he knew God couldn't lie. And it worried him. Ever since that day, Lucifer has been trying to destroy humanity. He enticed mankind deeper into sin until God was sick of it and decided to destroy all humanity except Noah and his family (Genesis 6:5–8).

When God chose Abraham out of all the men of his time and promised to bless him and make him a blessing, Lucifer attacked those people as well. Because he knew when God said He would make Abraham a blessing to the whole world, it was a repeat of the Genesis 3:15 promise.

I hope I haven't lost you. But in case I have, let me make it clear. Jesus was the one who would defeat Lucifer. Satan knew this. What he didn't know was when He would be born. But because of all the times God had repeated the promise since the Garden of Eden, he knew his destruction would come from the Jewish people and so he tried to destroy them.

The Jews should only have been in Babylon 70 years[1], but when the time had passed, many of them chose to remain because they were old, or because it was easier. The Jews became a divided people: some returned to Jerusalem while others remained in Media-Persia. Lucifer attacked both sets. The ones in Jerusalem faced their own challenges: enemies who wanted them to fail and tried to kill them, disease and famine. But God had a plan and His plans never fail.

I don't want you to think that because Jesus has already come to earth we are safe from the enmity of Lucifer. The Bible tells us:

> And the dragon was enraged with the woman, and he went to make war with the rest of her offspring, who keep the commandments of God and have the testimony of Jesus Christ (Revelation 12:17 NKJV).

In other words, Lucifer is still at war with humanity, particularly those who obey God and accept Jesus Christ as Lord and Savior. As queens-in-training, we have to remember we are always at war and we need to be battle ready. But, our enemy is not flesh and blood. So how do we fight an enemy we can't see? This is what Paul had to say about it:

> Finally, be strong in the Lord and in his mighty power. Put on the full armor of God, so that you can take your stand against the devil's schemes. For our struggle is not against flesh and blood, but against the rulers, against the authorities, against the powers of this dark world and against the spiritual forces of evil in the heavenly realms. Therefore put on the full armor of God, so that when the day of evil comes, you may be able to stand your ground, and after you have done everything, to stand.
>
> Stand firm then, with the belt of truth buckled around your waist, with the breastplate of righteousness in place, and with your feet fitted with the readiness that comes from the gospel of peace. In addition to all this, take up the shield of faith, with which you

can extinguish all the flaming arrows of the evil one. Take the helmet of salvation and the sword of the Spirit, which is the word of God.

And pray in the Spirit on all occasions with all kinds of prayers and requests. With this in mind, be alert and always keep on praying for all the Lord's people (Ephesians 6:10–18 NIV).

From these verses, we learn a number of things:

1. Our enemy is invisible.
2. He is powerful.
3. He can be defeated.
4. We have all that we need to defeat him.
5. It's important for us to stand firm.

God has given us everything we need to defeat the enemy, but it's important to note that we can't win unless we depend fully on God. Like Esther, our power comes from God. In Ephesians 6:8-10, Paul talked about the armor of God. He mentioned six key pieces of the armor—shoes, belt, breastplate, helmet, shield, and sword. He compared it to the gear of the Roman soldiers of his time because his audience would have been familiar with it. To make it more relatable, let's compare each tool to modern apparel where possible.

The Gospel Shoes

Many of us love shoes and can spend hours trying the find the right footwear for every occasion. We also know that wearing the wrong shoes can mean a very uncomfortable day for us. Most Roman soldiers were footmen. They had to walk everywhere and spent long hours on their feet on the battlefield. For that reason, they wore tough leather sandals which protected their feet. They also stuck nails through the base so they would stand firm on the different surfaces they fought on. The gospel shoes refer to the gospel of Christ. If we are not rooted and grounded in Jesus, we have no foundation or power.

The Belt of Truth

For the Roman soldier, the belt was one of the main pieces of their armor. It held a lot of equipment like a sword, ropes, and pouches for food rations. The belt was also instrumental for keeping the rest of the armor in place. The belt of Truth represents God who is Truth. What are we basing our lives on? How are we making decisions? Truth and integrity ought to be the basis of our characters.

The Breastplate of Righteousness

Isaiah says our righteousness is as filthy rags (Isaiah 64:6). So where do we get the ability to stand before God? Only people who are pure can stand in God's presence without being destroyed and the truth is, none of us meet that criteria. Only Jesus.

Jesus, the Son of God, who lived a perfect life and is willing to cover us in His righteousness. He takes on our filthiness so we can have the hope of ruling in heaven with God. The soldier's breastplate was attached to his belt with a series of leather thongs. It protected the chest—heart, lungs and other vital organs. How well do we guard ourselves against the influences of the world? What type of content (books, movies, music) do we feed regularly on?

The Helmet of Salvation

Okay, it's time for the helmet. I know—not the most attractive piece of clothing. But think of it this way: either we wear the helmet and protect our heads, or we ignore it and risk brain damage. The Roman soldier knew how important it was to protect his head from a blow to the skull. But if this is not a physical battle, what are we protecting our heads from?

We're protecting our mind. As we saw in the Garden of Eden, Lucifer uses words as his primary mode of attack. He plays a lot of word games. He says things that aren't true in such a way we wonder if he's telling the truth. Or, if we ever knew the truth in the first place. That's why we have to protect our minds.

Not everyone who talks about God is speaking about our Heavenly Father.

We do this by being careful of the things we watch, read and listen. The eyes and ears are the ways to the soul. That's how Satan influences us. Through books, music, movies, and conversation. We have to be careful to spend time feeding on the truth. This means listening to scripturally sound songs, the Bible and conversations that contain the truth.

If you are not sure what truth is, remember God is Truth. So it means then that any conversation with God at the center should be true. A word of caution though, not everyone who talks about God is speaking about our Heavenly Father. That's why you have to read the Bible for yourself. You need to make studying God's Word and praying a priority. If you don't know what the Bible says, how will you know what's true? Thankfully we have many apps that we can use to listen to the Bible.

The Shield of Faith

Our faith is our shield. The Roman shield was long and rectangular. It protected the soldier knee-to-chin from the arrows and spears of the enemy. It was big enough to hide behind when the enemy let off a barrage of arrows. We need faith to believe God when He says something. When we know who God is, we believe what He says. This will allow us to counteract Lucifer when he comes at us with lies.

The Sword of the Spirit

Being able to wield a sword took great strength. Thankfully, we're not being asked to lift anything heavier than our Bibles. As a queen-in-training, the Bible is your instruction manual. It will tell you how to address any situation you may encounter. It is also living and active. God's Word is applicable to you and the Holy Spirit will reveal it to you in a way that makes sense to you. That's how we access the true power[2].

You see, God has given us everything we need to be able to defeat the enemy. He doesn't expect us to do it on our own. In fact, He sets it up in such a way we have to depend on Him. Because he knows the enemy better than we ever can. And He has all the power in the universe to defeat him. Queens-in-training prepare for battle by always being in the Word and spending time in the presence of the Great King.

What are you feeding on?

What type of content are you reading, watching and listening?

I read my Bible...

a.   At least 15 minutes every day.
a.   5 minutes or more on most days.
b.   Once a week at church.
c.   Bible? I don't even know where mine is.

"I know the words to all the songs on the Top 100 Chart."

a.   That sounds exactly like me.
b.   Well, maybe not all of them, but most.
c.   I know the popular ones.
d.   I don't even know what the Top 100 Chart is.

I mostly read books that...

a.   Teach me how to live like Christ.
b.   Help me to become a better person.
c.   Are fun and entertaining.
d.   I only read magazines or tabloids.

If I invited God to go through my Netflix or YouTube feed, He'd see...

a.   Lots of programs that teach about Christ or Christian values.
b.   Clean movies and some programs that could be watched with my youth group at church.
c.   A lot of secular programs.
d.   What? I wouldn't let God go through my feed!

What are you feeding on?

What type of content are you reading, watching and listening?

Scoring:

Mostly As: Great job! You're living a Proverbs 4:23 life by guarding your mind. You understand that the content you consume will impact the person you become.

Mostly Bs: Consistency is a key skill for queens-in-training. The things we watch, listen and read teach lessons which become ingrained in our character.

Mostly Cs: This is an area you need to work on. Make a list of the type of books, music, programs, etc. that you consume regularly. Identify the ones that don't fit your identity as royalty.

Mostly Ds: Hmmm. What kind of story is your life telling? As ambassadors for Christ, we need to represent Him even when no one is looking. Doing this creates good habits that will remain with us forever.

11

My Relationship with God

*Q*ueen Esther is not mentioned once in chapter three yet many of the events will affect her. King Xerxes exalted Haman, one of his nobles, above all the others (Esther 3:1)—let's call him the new prime minister. The king commanded everyone in the kingdom to bow down before Haman. Everyone did—except Mordecai.

Why didn't Mordecai bow down? Wasn't he a Jew with a special obligation to represent God? If Mordecai was being a good steward, shouldn't he have obeyed the king's orders?

There are a lot of things happening here. Let's unpack some of them so you can get a better understanding.

Haman the Agagite

Some scholars believe Haman was a descendant of Amalekites. In Exodus 17:8–16, we read an interesting story which happened shortly after the Israelites left Egypt. The Amalekites attacked the children of Israel at Rephidim. The Israelites, under Joshua's leadership, fought back. Moses stood on a nearby hillside and watched the battle. As long as kept his hands raised, the Israelites triumphed over their enemies.

But when his hands got tired and he dropped them, the Israelites lost. Finally, he sat on a stone while Aaron and Hur held his hands up. At the end of that battle, God made a promise:

"Write this on a scroll as something to be remembered and make sure that Joshua hears it, because I will completely blot out the name of Amalek from under heaven" (Exodus 17:14 NIV).

Fast-forward a few hundred years and God was ready to destroy the Amalekites. The man he had chosen to do that was Saul, the first king of Israel. You can read the full story in 1 Samuel 15. God instructed Saul through Samuel the prophet to destroy the Amalekites and everything they owned. Saul and his army defeated the Amalekites, but they did not destroy all the possessions. And they did not kill Agag, the king.

You will remember that Haman was introduced as the son of Hammedatha, the Agagite (Esther 3:1). There are those who believe Haman was a descendant of that same king Agag[1]. Given the fact that God had ordered the Amalekites destroyed, it seems unlikely anyone survived the massacre of 1 Samuel 15.

It's about worship

A better explanation may have to do with what King Xerxes required his people to do. In our Bibles we read "reverence" or "pay honor", but let's look at the original language. The Hebrew word is shâchâh (pronounced shaw-khaw'). It means to depress, i.e. prostrate (especially reflexive, in homage to royalty or God), bow (self) down, crouch, fall

You're not too young to decide who you will worship.

down (flat), humbly beseech, do (make) obeisance, do reverence, make to stoop, worship[2]. You see, it wasn't just about showing honor to the new prime minister, it was about worship[3].

Jews were taught that only Jehovah is to be worshipped (Exodus 20:3–4). Mordecai refused to worship Haman. The choice of whom to worship is one every person has to make at some point in their lives. I hope you have already made the choice and have chosen to worship Jehovah.

You're not too young to decide on whom to worship. There is a great controversy with only two sides. In Revelation 12:7-17, we read about a great war in heaven. Even though it is described in physical terms, it is not a literal battle. You will not see the angels of God doing battle against the angels that have been cast out of heaven.

What you will experience is a spiritual battle (Ephesians 6:10–17). If you choose to serve God, you will be distracted from focusing on things which relate to Him by the things of this world. You will have things happen to you which you cannot explain. People will hate you without having any reason to do so. You will have to stand up for what you believe in many times and in various ways.

It's easy to get caught up in the physical and believe the person we see is our enemy, but that's not true. We may never see our real adversary. But that doesn't mean he doesn't exist. Don't fall for the lies which portray Satan as a red-skinned, horned, fork-tailed devil. This is what the Bible has to say about Lucifer:

"How you are fallen from heaven, O Day Star, son of Dawn!" (Isaiah 14:12 ESV)

And no wonder, for even Satan disguises himself as an angel of light (2 Corinthians 11:14 ESV).

"You were the signet of perfection, full of wisdom and perfect in beauty. You were in Eden, the garden of God; every precious stone was your covering, sardius, topaz, and diamond, beryl, onyx, and jasper, sapphire, emerald, and carbuncle; and crafted in gold were your settings and your engravings.

On the day that you were created they were prepared. You were an anointed guardian cherub. I placed you; you were on the holy mountain of God; in the midst of the stones of fire you walked" (Ezekiel 28:12-14 ESV).

Satan is beautiful! God made him perfect. But his character was less than stellar. He was blameless in every way until unrighteousness was found in him (Ezekiel 28:15).

Your heart was proud because of your beauty; you corrupted your wisdom for the sake of your splendor (Ezekiel 28:17 ESV).

He was a murderer from the beginning, and has nothing to do with the truth, because there is no truth in him. When he lies, he speaks out of his own character, for he is a liar and the father of lies (John 8:44 ESV).

Be sober-minded; be watchful. Your adversary the devil prowls around like a roaring lion, seeking someone to devour (1 Peter 5:8 ESV).

For some reason, Lucifer is determined to destroy humanity. I think it's because God chose to make us in His image and according to His likeness. The reason Satan hates us doesn't matter. The fact that he is determined to destroy you does.

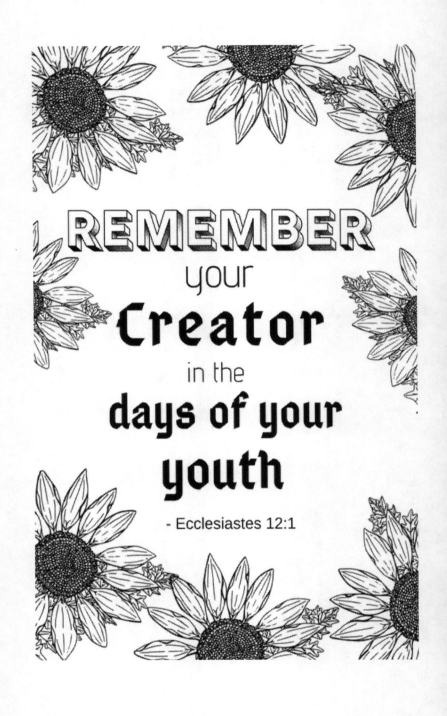

Like us, Lucifer was created with free will. He had a choice to serve God. But he became focused on his own beauty and made the choice to rebel against God. You also have a choice. You must make a decision about who you will serve. Which side are you on?

In case you are unsure who to choose, let me tell you some of the things the Bible has to say about God:

The twenty-four elders fall down before him who is seated on the throne and worship him who lives forever and ever. They cast their crowns before the throne, saying, "Worthy are you, our Lord and God, to receive glory and honor and power, for you created all things, and by your will they existed and were created" (Revelation 4:10–11 ESV).

Blessed be the God and Father of our Lord Jesus Christ, the Father of mercies and God of all comfort, who comforts us in all our affliction, so that we may be able to comfort those who are in any affliction, with the comfort with which we ourselves are comforted by God (2 Corinthians 1:3–4 ESV).

"Worthy are you, our Lord and God, to receive glory and honor and power, for you created all things, and by your will they existed and were created" (Revelation 4:11 ESV).

The God who made the world and everything in it, being Lord of heaven and earth, does not live in temples made by man, (Acts 17:24 ESV).

"For God so loved the world, that he gave his only Son, that whoever believes in him should not perish but have eternal life. For God did not send his Son into the world to condemn the world, but in order that the world might be saved through him" (John 3:16–17 ESV).

Who would you rather serve? The person who created you and every good thing in this world? Or, the person who is trying to destroy you and everyone whom you love?

Good and evil is played out all around us every day. We see it in nature. We experience it as a conflict in our inner self. We see it depicted in movies and books. Mordecai had a choice: he could prostrate himself before Haman and worship him as one worships God. Or, he could maintain his integrity knowing it may cost him his life. He chose to remain faithful to God.

As queens-in-training, sometimes we have to make hard choices. We have to do things that are unpopular because it's the right thing to do.

"Who knows if perhaps you were made queen for just such a time as this?" (Esther 4:14 NLT).

If Esther had been a vain woman I imagine these words would have deflated her a little. She had not been chosen queen because she was the most beautiful girl in the 127 provinces of Xerxes. She had not been chosen because she was the king's favorite. She had been chosen because her people needed someone who would be able to influence the king.

My reasons for serving God

. . . .

. . . .

. . . .

. . . .

. . . .

. . . .

. . . .

. . . .

. . . .

Sometimes it's hard for us to put the needs of others before ourselves. We have been socialized to believe that looking out for ourselves is the best thing to do. But you see, a good leader serves. They know what their people need and are willing to do what is necessary to ensure they receive it. We've talked about sacrifice and a leader's willingness to do what is best for the people they lead regardless of the cost to themselves. But what if the situation is too big for you to handle alone? What if there is nothing you, or anyone on earth, can do to change a situation? What then?

Esther had a situation she could not handle on her own. Her people had been targeted for destruction. If she said nothing, in about eleven months all of her people would be attacked, killed, and their possessions stolen. If she approached the king and he did not hold out the golden scepter, she would die (and her people would still be killed). What to do?

She called on God. Even though the book of Esther never once mentions His name, prayer, or the Holy Scriptures, it a story of God's love and care for His people. It is a story of God's Providence. For you to get the full picture of how God's protection is woven into this story, I have to tell you the Jewish people weren't supposed to be in Media-Persia at that time.

Hundreds of years earlier, God had warned His people through His prophets that if they did not stop worshiping idols He would drive them from the Promised Land as captives.

"This is what the Lord Almighty, the God of Israel, says: I will put an iron yoke on the necks of all these nations to make them serve Nebuchadnezzar king of Babylon, and they will serve him. I will even give him control over the wild animals"' (Jeremiah 28:13 NIV).

Therefore the Lord Almighty says this: "Because you have not listened to my words, I will summon all the peoples of the north and my servant Nebuchadnezzar king of Babylon," declares the Lord, "and I will bring them against this land and its inhabitants and against all the surrounding nations. I will completely destroy them and make them an object of horror and scorn, and an everlasting ruin. I will banish from them the sounds of joy and gladness, the voices of bride and bridegroom, the sound of millstones and the light of the lamp. This whole country will become a desolate wasteland, and these nations will serve the king of Babylon seventy years.

"But when the seventy years are fulfilled, I will punish the king of Babylon and his nation, the land of the Babylonians, for their guilt," declares the Lord, "and will make it desolate forever" (Jeremiah 25:8–12 NIV).

The Israelites didn't obey so they were captured by King Nebuchadnezzar and taken to Babylon. The first expedition to Jerusalem was in 605-604 BC[4]. At first, the king of Babylon allowed the majority of the Israelites to remain in their land and assigned a designate. However, because of numerous uprisings, the majority of Jews were taken to Babylon. This happened in three separate deportations[5]. The Jews were very attached to their land and the Temple in which the Lord dwelt. Being taken away from their beloved land and their beloved Temple could have been discouraging for them. It could have caused many to believe God no longer loved them or considered them His special people.

But woven in the midst of their chastisement was the promise of redemption and a return to the land they loved so much.

This is what the LORD says: "You will be in Babylon for seventy years. But then I will come and do for you all the good things I have promised, and I will bring you home again" (Jeremiah 29:10 NLT).

In 539 BC, King Cyrus the Great of Persia conquered Babylon[6]. In 538 BC, King Cyrus granted permissions for the Israelites to return to Jerusalem to rebuild the Temple[7].

In the first year of Cyrus king of Persia, in order to fulfill the word of the Lord spoken by Jeremiah, the Lord moved the heart of Cyrus king of Persia to make a proclamation throughout his realm and also to put it in writing:

"This is what Cyrus king of Persia says:

"'The Lord, the God of heaven, has given me all the kingdoms of the earth and he has appointed me to build a temple for him at Jerusalem in Judah. Any of his people among you may go up to Jerusalem in Judah and build the temple of the Lord, the God of Israel, the God who is in Jerusalem, and may their God be with them. And in any locality where survivors may now be living, the people are to provide them with silver and gold, with goods and livestock, and with freewill offerings for the temple of God in Jerusalem.'"

Then the family heads of Judah and Benjamin, and the priests and Levites—everyone whose heart God had moved—prepared to go up and build the house of the Lord in Jerusalem (Ezra 1:1–5 NIV).

I bet you're thinking I'm bad at math since the difference between 605 and 538 is not 70. How could the Jews have been in captivity 70 years when Math tells us it had only been 67 years? It has a lot to do with the Jewish calendar.

The Jews maintained a lunar calendar where each month started with a new moon. This resulted in a year that was about twelve days shorter than our average year[8]. Additionally, their calendar began in the spring and not in January as our does. Furthermore, according to Jewish reckoning, any part of a year can count as a full year[9].

But not many of them returned. Not many people wanted to return to a land that had been ravaged by war and wild animals. They had settled into Media-Persia, build homes and businesses. They didn't want to uproot their family to take them to a country they had only heard about in stories. The ones who remembered Jerusalem would have been too

> When we know who God is, we will be able to discern His voice.

old to travel. The Jews didn't want to leave comfort for uncertainty, danger, and ruin. So they remained in Persia[6].

Here was another opportunity for God to say, "See, you were disobedient and so I will allow you to reap what you have sown." But He didn't do that. He lovingly put plans in place to care for His people who were in the wrong place at the wrong time.

Only God could have arranged the unique set of circumstances which led to Esther's coronation. Only God could have arranged for Esther to be taken among the virgins and granted her the favor of the king and everyone she came in contact with.

Esther knew the Lord. She had an intimate relationship with Him and so was able to call on Him when she needed help. A woman who did not know God would have tried to sway the king on the merit of her own actions. And maybe that would have saved her life, but I doubt it would have been enough to save an entire nation.

Tips for Bible Study

As queens-in-training, we have to know the King of kings. We have to spend time in His presence before the big, challenging things of our lives happen. When we know who God is, we will be able to discern His voice. We will do what He wants us to do. How much time are you spending with Him? How often do you pray, read your Bible or just sit quietly listening for His voice?

If you're struggling to study the Bible, here are a few tips:

1. Give yourself enough time to study. Schedule a specific time for your time with God. Treat this time as it is sacred. Ensure that you have enough uninterrupted time to spend in the Word. For each person, this will be different. Figure out the best time of day for you to spend with your Heavenly Father.

2. Organize your study area. Get everything you need. If you know you need sixteen pens, a drink of water and three

notebooks, make sure you have them. Assembly those ahead of time so that you have everything you need at hand. It may be a good idea to have somewhere to store everything like a basket or a bag.

3. Use different techniques and methods. While it is true that we want to be good students of the Word, it's also true that sometimes we get jaded in our study. We lose the excitement and things begin to feel...boring. Try different techniques of study.

Suggestions for studying the Bible are by chapters, books or verse by verse. You can also choose a Bible character and study all the texts related to that person. This series of videos on YouTube will introduce you to various ways to study your Bible: http://bit.ly/Bible4Beginners.

4. Teach someone what you know. One of the best ways to cement new knowledge is to share it. Share the information with someone. Did you get a new understanding of a parable? Tell at least one person. Did you finally figure out what an obscure text means? Share it with a friend.

5. Study with a group. Find a group of persons who are as enthusiastic about learning more about God as you are. Meet regularly to study the Bible. Include family members or siblings in your Bible study time.

6. Meditate. Spend time thinking about what you have studied. What new thing did you learn about God? What was confirmed? What stuck with you? How will this knowledge change the way you do things?

How do I spend my time?

School/work...

Homework..

Chores..

Screen time..

Sleep...

With friends...

Praying...

Reading my Bible...

At church...

Other activities..

It's important also for us to realize that studying the Bible is totally different from reading it. Believers should read the Bible daily, but should also make time to do an in-depth study of the word of God. We are called to "study to show ourselves approved" (2 Timothy 2:15)[10]. As queens-in-training, we need to become skilled Bible scholars as we seek to learn more about the God who sent His only Son to save humanity from sin.

12

The Right Way to Fight

*T*riumph for the Jews came when they were given permission to defend themselves against their enemies. A lot of people died before those who hated the Jews stopped attacking them. What does that mean for us today? Is it right for us to kill if we are attacked first?

Let's talk a little about the Ten Commandments. You may already know what they are and be familiar with the background against which they were given, but let's talk about it anyway. (I want to make sure both of us have the same understanding before we move on).

After God saved the Israelites from their Egyptian slave masters, they spent some time at Mount Sinai learning how God wanted them to behave. These instructions were condensed into Ten Commandments written on two tablets of stone. These were the commandments in a nutshell:

- Don't have any other gods except Jehovah.

- Don't make idols or bow down and serve them because God is jealous.

- Do not take the name of the Lord your God in vain.

- Remember the Sabbath day, to keep it holy. We should only work six days because the seventh belongs to God and is reserved for worship.

- Honor your father and your mother so that you'll have a long life.

- Do not murder.

- Do not commit adultery.

- Do not steal.

- Do not bear false witness against your neighbor. (Don't say they did something when they didn't.)

- Don't envy others for what they have.

You can read the full verbiage in Exodus 20:1–17. The commandments are basically divided into two categories. One category applies to God and how He wants to be worshipped. The other applies to mankind and how we should treat each other.

"You shall not murder[1]" is the sixth commandment, the second of the set which deals with our treatment of each other. And this is not the only thing the God had to say about murder:

"Whoever takes a human life shall surely be put to death" (Leviticus 24:17 ESV).

Beloved, never avenge yourselves, but leave it to the wrath of God, for it is written, "Vengeance is mine, I will repay, says the Lord" (Romans 12:19 ESV).

You are of your father the devil, and your will is to do your father's desires. He was a murderer from the beginning, and has nothing to do with the truth, because there is no truth in him. When he lies, he speaks out of his own character, for he is a liar and the father of lies (John 8:44 ESV).

"He will wipe away every tear from their eyes, and death shall be no more, neither shall there be mourning, nor crying, nor pain anymore, for the former things have passed away" (Revelation 21:4 ESV).

A time to kill, and a time to heal; a time to break down, and a time to build up; (Ecclesiastes 3:3 ESV).

"But as for the cowardly, the faithless, the detestable, as for murderers, the sexually immoral, sorcerers, idolaters, and all liars, their portion will be in the lake that burns with fire and sulfur, which is the second death" (Revelation 21:8 ESV).

We read these verses, and many others, and realize that God is serious about this business of us killing each other. But why did He allow the Jews to kill more than 75 thousand people? Was that some sort of double standard?

I understand how confused you may feel when you see bad things happen even while you're told (or believe) God is good. If God is so good, why would He allow His people to kill? Why do bad things happen? There's only one answer: sin.

When God created the earth, it was perfect. Mankind lived in harmony with animals and nature. Every creature—even man—were vegetarians because there was no death in the Garden of Eden. Unfortunately, our forefathers sinned and because of sin, bad things happen.

The beautiful thing is that even while bad things happen, God continues to show His great love for humanity, by the way He treats us. Because of the death of His Son Jesus, we have the opportunity to repent of our sins and receive forgiveness.

Before Jesus came to earth, God had put plans in place for His people to repent and receive forgiveness. The sacrificial system laid out in the book of Leviticus foreshadowed Jesus' death and what it would mean for humanity[2].

By 479 BC[3], the Jews were very familiar with this system. They knew the value God placed on human life and did not take it lightly. Not until they were given permission to defend themselves did they fight back. The Jews knew they were God's chosen people and that He would deliver them out of their predicament. In this case, God gave them permission to defend themselves.

As queen-in-training, we need to recognize the value God places on the life of every human being, it doesn't matter who they are or what they've done.

"Do you think that I like to see wicked people die? says the Sovereign LORD. Of course not! I want them to turn from their wicked ways and live" (Ezekiel 18:23 NLT).

He values and loves each of us and wants us to be saved. It is in light of this love I want you to take the lesson of this chapter. God doesn't want you to be bullied and treated poorly. But He doesn't want you to bully anyone or treat them unkindly either. And this, my dear friend, is where things get tricky. How do we fight back and not sin?

Remember what Esther did? She didn't do anything to defend herself or her people before she consulted God. When you find yourself in a position where you need to fight back, you have to control yourself and not to give in to the urge. Ask God how you should handle it. This can be a quick, whispered prayer. But what happens when you pray about something for a while and nothing happens? The first thing you have to check is if you're praying the right way (yes, there is a wrong and right way for you to pray). If you are, it may be that you need to fast to receive the answer to your prayer.

The Right Way to Pray

Prayer is a request for help or an expression of thanks addressed to our Heavenly Father. It's a way of connecting with Him and a source of receiving power. When we talk to God, we tell Him what we desire or hope for. We don't pray because we want to tell God what's happening in our lives— He already knows. We pray because we want to strengthen our relationship with Him.

The Bible has a lot to say about prayer so we'll focus on some of the basic principles of effective prayer.

My prayer requests

1. Acknowledge the Sovereignty of God. Remember who you're praying to. We can sometimes forget that God is the Creator of the universe and everything in it—including us. When you pray, approach Him with reverence and humility.

2. God answers our prayers according to His will—understand that God is able to do anything, even things which seem impossible. He answers prayers the way He chooses and not necessarily the way we want Him to (1 John 5:14).

3. God hears our prayers and will answer them when we humbly seek Him and turn from our wicked ways. God is not our enabler. He will not reward us for bad behavior. It means, therefore, before we seek God's face to make a request, we need to repent of our sins and take on the righteousness of Christ (2 Chronicles 7:14, 1 John 5:15).

4. We should pray in every season of our lives. Some of us only pray when we're in trouble. That's not what God wants (James 5:13). Think of it this way: imagine you had a friend who only reached out to you when she had a problem, would you consider her a good friend? That's what we do to God; we ignore Him until we're in trouble and need help.

5. Pray and believe you will receive an answer. Have you ever asked your parents for something you knew you weren't going to get? Don't take that approach when praying. If you're asking according to God's will, be confident that He will grant you as you ask (Matthew 11:24).

6. Pray sincerely and succinctly. There are many people who pray long, eloquent prayers. If that's you, keep on doing what you do. But recognize that it's not the eloquence or length of a prayer that gets God's attention. It's the state of your relationship (Matthew 6:7). If you're not a person who prays long prayers, don't be intimidated by those who do. God knows your heart and will respond accordingly.

7. Make your request specific. If you make a rambling request, how will you know when God has answered your prayer? Be clear in what you're asking for and make sure you ask for what you want. No, they're not the same thing. You see, sometimes we ask for something and when we get it we realize that's not what we wanted in the first place. Think about what you want and make your request clear to God.

8. Worship and praise God when you have received an answer. Don't forget to say thanks. Our thanksgiving should start before God answers our prayers. Even if the answer is no, God is still God.

9. Testify about answered prayers. Be sure to tell your family and friends what God has done for you. Write down the prayers God answers so you can reflect on them. This is especially helpful when you're going through a difficult time. Reading about the times God answered your prayer will remind you how much He loves you and what He has done for you.

PRAISE

REPENT

ASK

YIELD

Remember to P.R.A.Y.

A fun way to approach prayer is to remember the acronym P.R.A.Y.

Praise God for what He has done and who He is. Start with praise or worship. This can be in the form of a song or prayer chorus. Or, you may quote Scriptures which talk about the attributes of God and why He is worthy of our praise.

Repent of your sins. Try to remember any sins you've committed and sincerely ask God to forgive you for them. You can also ask the Holy Spirit to remind you of any unconfessed sins so that you can ask for forgiveness.

Ask for what you want. Make your request. Tell God what you would like Him to do. Be clear and specific with your request.

Yield. Acknowledge His right to answer as He sees fit. Even if God doesn't answer your prayer the way you wanted Him to, He is still God and worthy of praise.

How to Fast

We had hinted at this in earlier chapters, but let's go into some more detail. Fasting is when we give something up—usually food—in order to draw closer to God. We can also give up things like movies, reading, social media or a certain food (like junk food) for a specified period. Spend the time you'd normally do those activities with God.

When we decide to fast we have to first make sure we're doing it for the right reasons. Are you fasting because you think you can force (or persuade) God to do what you want Him to do? If that's what you're thinking, your heart's in the wrong place. Some biblical reasons for fasting include:

- To receive an answer from God
- For healing
- For protection
- For deliverance for ourselves or someone else
- Before making decisions
- Before starting a ministry
- For spiritual strength
- As an act of repentance for our sins
- When we're in the midst of a trial

God knows our hearts and He is always available to help us through our struggles.

When we're fasting, our focus should be on God and not the thing we're giving up. In the book of Esther, the Jews fasted because they wanted deliverance for themselves and for their people. They weren't trying to manipulate God, they just wanted Him to know they needed His help badly enough to give up something important—food and water.

So what happens after you fast and pray but there's still no response from God? Do we allow ourselves to be treated poorly by others? Or, do we seek revenge on them for what they've done to us?

We have to remember that we already know the right thing to do. The whole point of our life is to be an ambassador for Christ. Take a moment and think about it: what would a queen do? As queens-in-training, our behavior should never reflect poorly on our Heavenly Father (it will happen sometimes but it's not our aim). The beauty is that God knows our hearts and He is always available to help us through our struggles.

Last Words

Whew! That was a lot of stuff. We're now at the end of our in-depth study of the book of Esther. I hope you've learned a lot about what it means to be a royal (or a queen-in-training as we've been calling it). And that you've gleaned an idea of the skills you need to become the best queen-in-training you can be.

Just to recap, here are some of the things we covered:

- How to be an ambassador for Christ
- Anyone can be queen as long as they meet certain criteria
- Choosing the right attitude
- Honoring our parents
- Respecting those set over us
- Treating our peers with respect

- Honoring God
- Cultivating a culture of care
- Discerning what's right
- Dealing with pride and prejudice
- Choosing good friends
- Dealing with anger
- Learning to forgive
- Overcoming fear
- Dealing with the real enemy
- Deciding who to worship
- Tips for studying the Bible
- The right way to pray
- How to fast

My hope is that Esther has encouraged you to draw closer to God and to appreciate the person you are while learning to treat others with respect. You saw a young woman who was taken from her family and thrust into a completely different lifestyle yet somehow was able to thrive.

Esther's story can be yours too (no, you won't be forced to marry a king and become the queen of a vast empire, at least, I hope not). But, you can choose to have a positive attitude regardless of the circumstances you find yourself in. You're already royal now all you have to do is choose:

You can choose to be brave. And to do brave things even when you're scared.

You can choose to serve God with all your heart.

You can choose to be a better version of yourself today and every day from now on.

Go, my dear queen-in-training, I'm praying for you.

Father, I pray for _____. You know her heart and how she longs to be an ambassador for You. You see her challenges and the obstacles in her way,

You know what discourages and what gives her a little more drive to press on. I pray that You will help her through the challenges and obstacles in her way.

Teach her when she needs to grab hold of Your strength and push through, and when You want her to go in another direction. Help her to submit every area of her life to You so that one day she will reign with You in heaven. In Jesus' name, I pray. Amen.

***

Thank you for taking the time to read Royal: Life Lessons from the Book of Esther. If you enjoyed this book would you consider leaving a review on Amazon or Goodreads? Your feedback is a great asset for getting this book into the hands of more readers like you.

A Gift for You

I've created a set of ten coloring pages for you.

You can download them for free when you join my newsletter through this link: http://bit.ly/RoyalPages.

Read on for an
excerpt of book 2 in the

Girls of Excellence
Series

Beloved Excerpt

One

*J*ohn's Gospel tells an interesting story. A woman was caught in adultery and brought before Jesus. Adultery, according to the Bible, is sexual intimacy between a woman who is married or betrothed and a man who is not her husband or bethrothed[1]. This sin was punishable by death according to Mosaic Law. The scribes and Pharisees wanted her to be put to death according to the law. Let's read her story in John 8:2-11:

Now early in the morning He came again into the temple, and all the people came to Him; and He sat down and taught them. Then the scribes and Pharisees brought to Him a woman caught in adultery. And when they had set her in the midst, they said to Him, "Teacher, this woman was caught in adultery, in the very act. Now Moses, in the law, commanded us that such should be stoned. But what do You say?" This they said, testing Him, that they might have something of which to accuse Him. But Jesus stooped down and wrote on the ground with His finger, as though He did not hear.

So when they continued asking Him, He raised Himself up and said to them, "He who is without sin among you, let him throw a stone at her first." And again He stooped down and wrote on the ground. Then those who heard it, being convicted by their conscience, went out one by one, beginning with the oldest even to the last. And Jesus was left alone, and the woman standing in the midst. When Jesus had raised Himself up and saw no one but the woman, He said to her, "Woman, where are those accusers of yours? Has no one condemned you?"

She said, "No one, Lord."

And Jesus said to her, "Neither do I condemn you; go and sin no more" (NKJV).

So I know you have questions. Let me answer some of them, and then, we'll dig into the story to find the lesson.

Who were the scribes?

The word translated as scribe is the Greek grammateús, (pronounced gram-mat-yooce') and it simply means a writer, i.e. (professionally) scribe or secretary, scribe, town-clerk[2].

An examination of Bible text uncovers three different types of scribes.

1. Kings had scribes. These were men who were responsible for denoting important events in the life of the king as seen in Esther 8:9 and 1 Chronicles 24:5-7.

2. A person skilled in the Mosaic Law and the commandments as seen in Ezra 7:6, 11. This person was able to read and explain the law (Nehemiah 8:1).

3. A military scribe. This person was responsible for keeping a list of the officers and men in a military unit (also

known as a muster roll) or prison as seen in Jeremiah 37:15, 20 and Jeremiah 52:25.

Based on the context, we can determine that the scribes mentioned in John 8 are men who had training in reading and understanding Mosaic Law.

Who were the Pharisees?

The word translated as Pharisee is the Greek word Pharisaîos, (pronounced far-is-ah'-yos). The word is of Hebrew origin and could also mean a separatist, i.e. exclusively religious, a Pharisean, i.e. Jewish sectary[3]. So you may be wondering is who were the Pharisees separating themselves from? But more on that in a minute, first I want to give you some more information about them.

It's interesting to note that there were no Pharisees in the Old Testament. I find that significant as their main purpose seemed to be advising the Jews how to keep the Mosaic Law to the minutest detail. Historians believe the group was formed after the Jewish exile[4].

Pharisees believed in the existence of good and evil angels, and in the coming Messiah. They also believed that the dead, after a period of either reward or penalty in Hades, would be resurrected by the Messiah. They would be rewarded according to their actions[5].

The Pharisees show up in the New Testament as a group of men who followed the law to such an extent they considered it sin to heal a person on the Sabbath[6]. Yet, they were more concerned with appearances than living a godly life. These same men plotted to kill Jesus on the Sabbath and thought nothing of it (Matthew 12:14).

As we read about the Pharisees, we get a clear picture that what they wanted separation from was anyone who did not agree with them or live as they did. Jesus seemed to be very scathing about them during His ministry. These are some of the things He said to or about them:

Therefore anyone who sets aside one of the least of these commands and teaches others accordingly will be called least in the kingdom of heaven, but whoever practices and teaches these commands will be called great in the kingdom of heaven. For I tell you that unless your righteousness surpasses that of the Pharisees and the teachers of the law, you will certainly not enter the kingdom of heaven (Matthew 5:19-21 NIV).

"Woe to you, teachers of the law and Pharisees, you hypocrites! You travel over land and sea to win a single convert, and when you have succeeded, you make them twice as much a child of hell as you are.

"Woe to you, blind guides! You say, 'If anyone swears by the temple, it means nothing; but anyone who swears by the gold of the temple is bound by that oath' (Matthew 23:14-16 NIV).

"Woe to you, teachers of the law and Pharisees, you hypocrites! You give a tenth of your spices—mint, dill and cumin. But you have neglected the more important matters of the law— justice, mercy and faithfulness. You should have practiced the latter, without neglecting the former. You blind guides! You strain out a gnat but swallow a camel (Matthew 23:23-24 NIV).

"Woe to you, teachers of the law and Pharisees, you hypocrites! You shut the door of the kingdom of heaven in people's faces. You yourselves do not enter, nor will you let those enter who are trying to (Matthew 23:13 NIV).

216

"The teachers of the law and the Pharisees sit in Moses' seat. So you must be careful to do everything they tell you. But do not do what they do, for they do not practice what they preach" (Matthew 23:2-3 NIV).

Jesus called the scribes and Pharisees hypocrites. This was the Greek word hypokritḗs, (pronounced hoop-ok-ree-tace') which meant actor under an assumed character (stage-player), i.e. (figuratively) a dissembler, hypocrite[7]. As far as Jesus was concerned, they were playing a role and should not be believed.

What is adultery?

Today, we define adultery as sexual intercourse between a married person and a person who is not their spouse[8]. But the Bible simply defines adultery as sex with another man's wife (Leviticus 20:10). In other words, if one of the two people engaged in sexual intercourse was married, they committed adultery. Both persons were considered adulterers.

What is the punishment for adultery?

The punishment for both the adulterer and adulteress was death by stoning.

"If a man is found lying with a woman married to a husband, then both of them shall die—the man that lay with the woman, and the woman; so you shall put away the evil from Israel" (Deuteronomy 22:22 NKJV).

Wow! I know. And you may be wondering why was the punishment for adultery so harsh. Well, God doesn't really want anyone to be killed. He would have preferred if everyone would obey His commandments. His law was put in place for our benefit, not His.

God made sure to tell the Israelites they should not commit adultery. He was so serious about it He made it the seventh commandment (Exodus 20:14). When God created marriage it was meant to be an intimate and lasting bond between a man and a woman. Intimacy in marriage is lost when persons are not faithful to each other. Besides, there are other emotions that can be aroused because of an adulterous union. Things like anger, jealousy, hate…it's a long list and I'm sure you can think of a lot more.

God knew all the consequences for unfaithfulness in marriage and He wanted to protect His people from them. He had seen the effects of it in the years after Adam and Eve had disobeyed Him and eaten from the tree of life.

After God told the Israelites not to commit adultery, He went into great detail about what amounted to sexual sin. You can read all about it in Leviticus 20:10-31. But I don't want you to misunderstand and think people could just go around stoning each other to death. There was a process. When a man or woman was accused of adultery there would be a hearing. They were brought before the elders in the presence of at least two witnesses:

Whoever is deserving of death shall be put to death on the testimony of two or three witnesses; he shall not be put to death on the testimony of one witness. The hands of the witnesses shall be the first against him to put him to death, and afterward the hands of all the people. So you shall put away the evil from among you (Deuteronomy 17:6-7 NKJV).

In that way, it was similar to a modern court of law. Guilty persons were tried by a jury of their peers and sentenced. Some sins carried a death penalty and adultery was one of them.

The Background

According to the men who brought the adulteress to Jesus, she had been "caught in the very act". Two persons were involved in the act, this woman and the man who was not her spouse. Yet, only one person was brought to stand trial. According to Mosaic Law, both persons were punishable by death. Why then did the scribes and Pharisees bring the woman while allowing the man to go free?

Unfortunately, that question was not answered in Scripture. But, even without an answer, there are many things we can learn from this story. Before we start unpacking the lessons, let's look a little at the background.

In the previous chapter of John we read these interesting words:

After this, Jesus went around in Galilee. He did not want to go about in Judea because the Jewish leaders there were looking for a way to kill him (John 7:1 NIV).

Jesus had His own problems. He had to avoid certain places because the Jewish leaders were trying to kill Him. In fact, the night before at the Feast of Tabernacles, there had been a failed attempt to capture Him. After spending the night on Mount Olive, Jesus was at the Temple teaching the people. It was at this moment that the scribes and Pharisees brought the woman to Jesus.

A woman condemned to death. Standing before the man who claimed to be the Son of God. Surely, God would want to uphold the law, wouldn't He?

Threefold Grace

Jesus' response to the woman shows us how God responds to His children when we sin. But there are other lessons about grace in that story, let's unpack all of them.

God's grace

The story of the woman caught in adultery is one of grace. She received the unmerited favor of God. Jesus knew what she had done was punishable by death according to Mosaic Law—so did she. So imagine her surprise when Jesus said: "let he who is without sin cast the first stone" (John 8:7).

That was not how it worked. It was the witnesses who were to cast the first stones. According to Mosaic Law, a person could only be condemned or accused if there were at least two witnesses. These witnesses would be the first to begin stoning the accused.

Since she had been caught in the act of adultery, there must have been witnesses, right? So why didn't Jesus tell the witnesses to stone her? It was because of grace. Jesus was trying to teach the scribes and Pharisees--as well as, the people looking on--that a person's guilt doesn't equate to condemnation. Forgiveness—grace—is always an option, because where sin abounds, grace abounds much more.

Grace towards others

The scribes and Pharisees wanted God Jesus to condemn the woman to death. They had no concern about her life or who she may be leaving behind. They weren't even concerned that the man with whom she had been caught in the act, had been left behind. They only wanted what they considered justice. They wanted to rid the world of her presence. Period.

As religious leaders, they should have been more compassionate. They should have been more loving but all they wanted was her to be punished. But Jesus refused to give them the justice they sought. He had wanted them to realize that she was a human being just as they were. Jesus wanted them to realize that while the woman had sinned, they forgive her. They had the chance to offer grace to this adulteress.

God is always concerned with the way we treat others. He's always concerned with the way we offer forgiveness to persons. That's why He told us the way we forgive others is the way He will forgive us. If we are unwilling to forgive, then God will mimic our behavior. Not because He doesn't want to forgive us, but because He's hoping to teach us. Sin carries a death penalty but the only person worthy to judge is God.

Grace towards self

After Jesus had told the scribes and Pharisees that the first person without sin should cast the first stone, they were convicted by their consciences and walked away. Jesus looked at her and saw her need. He knew she needed forgiveness and so He offered it to her freely. His response was "I don't condemn you, go and sin no more". In other words, she had been given a second chance, she had literally received a second life. Her sin which should have resulted in her death hadn't. Now she had an opportunity to make different choices. She could live basking in the love of her Heavenly Father who had forgiven her after she had sinned against Him.

But here's the thing, living this new life required grace. Her peers knew her sin. She would have to walk among those who knew her as an adulteress. Some of them wouldn't forgive her. Some of them wouldn't allow her to forget what she had done and she'd have to live with that. She'd have to learn to accept the forgiveness Jesus had given her so freely. She'd have to embrace it and learn to live forgiven.

Beloved, I want you to learn a lesson from this woman. When God forgives you He doesn't take it back. All He asks is that you turn away from the sin you had committed and sin no more. Does God know that sometimes it will be difficult and you'd fall into the same sin many times? Yes. But He's willing to forgive you every time. If you ask Him to.

If we confess our sins, He is faithful and just to forgive us our sins and to cleanse us from all unrighteousness (1 John 1:9 NKJV).

As long as you repent and ask for forgiveness, God will forgive you and offer you grace. Don't condemn yourself for sin God has already forgiven.

Acknowledgements

MC and DC, I'm always touched by how supportive you are of my work. I appreciate the days (and nights) you listened to me plan, read or just talk about this project.

Special thanks to the Kingdom Bloggers who supported me through the process.

Denise, as always, your calls to check on my progress helped to keep me accountable throughout the process. I'm so grateful for your friendship.

I'm grateful for every person who read, commented or provided feedback on this book. It became a stronger piece of work because of it.

To my Heavenly Father, none of this would have been possible without You. I need Your strength daily and appreciate the way You teach me even as You inspire me to write.

Notes

CHAPTER 1: WHAT A QUEEN IS NOT

1. Some Bible translations call him Ahasuerus instead of Xerxes. We'll refer to him as Xerxes for the rest of this book for ease of pronunciation.

2. The Pulpit Commentary, Electronic Database. Copyright © 2001, 2003, 2005, 2006, 2010 by BibleSoft, Inc., Used by permission

3. Benson Commentary on the Old and New Testaments, Text Courtesy of BibleSupport.com. Used by Permission.

4. Some translations call them eunuchs instead of chamberlains. A eunuch was a man who had been castrated. This was usually done early enough in his life for him to have had hormonal changes. Because these men were not able to father children, they were sometimes trusted to guard the harems of kings or high officials.

Eunuch https://en.wikipedia.org/wiki/Eunuch,

Eunuch https://www.biblestudytools.com/dictionary/eunuch/

Notes

5. Depose means to remove (someone) from office suddenly and forcefully.

6. Distance from Ethiopia to India, https://www.distancefromto.net/distance-from-ethiopia-to-india

7. Greco-Persian Wars, The Editors of Encyclopaedia Britannica, LAST UPDATED: Mar 18, 2019, Encyclopædia Britannica, Publisher: Encyclopædia Britannica, Inc. https://www.britannica.com/event/Greco-Persian-Wars,

8. Expositions of Holy Scripture, Alexander MacLaren, Text Courtesy of BibleSupport.com. Used by Permission.

9. Exposition of the Entire Bible by John Gill [1746-63]. Text Courtesy of Internet Sacred Texts Archive.

10. Jamieson, Fausset, and Brown in A Commentary, Critical, Experimental and Practical on the Old and New Testaments

11. NLT Chronological Life Application Study Bible, Tyndale House Publishers, Inc. (November 2, 2012) page 1183

12. Memucan was the chief prince who suggested that all the women in the kingdom would use Esther's example as an excuse to disobey their husbands (Esther 1:16-20).

Some Bible translations have this name spelt Memukan.

13. Shortly after God delivered the Israelites from Egypt—He taught them that they were to be His priests and a holy nation (Exodus 19:6).

14. Revelation 1:6 and Revelation 5:10 also make reference to the kings and priests of God reigning with Him in heaven or on the new earth.

CHAPTER 2: CHARACTERISTICS OF A QUEEN

1. Notes on the Bible by Albert Barnes [1834]. Text Courtesy of Internet Sacred Texts Archive.

2. A harem is a place where wives and concubines (secondary wives or mistresses) live.

3. In Esther 8:8, King Xerxes tells Mordecai his new Prime Minister that he needs to write a new decree to save his people because once the king writes a decree it cannot be reversed.

4. Some of the concubines would have been captives from other lands. Persian monarchs were known to maintain, besides their legitimate wives, as many as 300 or 400 concubines (compare Esther 2:14). Notes on the Bible by Albert Barnes [1834]. Text Courtesy of Internet Sacred Texts Archive.

5. The Bachelor is an hour-long TV series where a single bachelor dates 25 women over several weeks. By the end of the series, the hope is that he would have found his true love. The series was first aired in 2002. The Bachelor, http://www.tv.com/shows/the-bachelor/

6. Benson Commentary on the Old and New Testaments, Text Courtesy of BibleSupport.com. Used by Permission.

7. Benson Commentary on the Old and New Testaments, Text Courtesy of BibleSupport.com. Used by Permission.

8. Exposition of the Entire Bible by John Gill [1746-63]. Text Courtesy of Internet Sacred Texts Archive.

9. Benson Commentary on the Old and New Testaments, Text Courtesy of BibleSupport.com. Used by Permission.

10. Orr, James, M.A., D.D. General Editor. "Entry for 'ASHTORETH'". "International Standard Bible Encyclopedia". 1915. https://www.biblestudytools.com/dictionary/ashtoreth/

11. Babylon, https://en.wikipedia.org/wiki/Babylon#Persian_conquest

12. Eastern kings' usually renamed captives after the names of their pagan gods. A similar practice is seen in Daniel 1 where the four Hebrew boys were renamed after being appointed to the king's palace.

13. One of Abraham's descendant was a man named Jacob whom God renamed Israel. Jacob had 12 sons: Reuben, Simeon, Levi, Judah, Dan, Naphtali, Gad, Asher, Issachar, Zebulun, Joseph, and Benjamin (Genesis 35:22-36). Each of his sons became the father of one of the twelve tribes of Israel. There is no tribe named after his son Joseph. Instead, there are two tribes Manasseh and Ephraim named for Joseph's two sons who were adopted by Jacob. The Levites were not given a traditional allotment as they were given the portion which belonged to God.

14. Who Is a Jew? Judaism 101, Tracey R Rich, http://www.jewfaq.org/whoisjew.htm

15. I found this video on the ceremonial washing of hands enlightening: https://www.youtube.com/watch?v=FAAlzSZU-Rw

16. Esther, Seventh-day Adventist Bible Commentary Volume 3, Edited by Francis D. Nichol, Hagerstown Review and Herald Publishing Association (1954)

17. Babylonian Exile, The Editors of Encyclopaedia Britannica, Encyclopædia Britannica, Publisher: Encyclopædia Britannica, Inc. Date Published: December 27, 2017,

https://www.britannica.com/event/Babylonian-Exile, Access Date: March 29, 2019

18. "H2896 - towb - Strong's Hebrew Lexicon (KJV)." No Pages. Cited 29 Mar 2019. https://www.blueletterbible.org//lang/lexicon/lexicon.cfm?Strongs=H2896&t=KJV.

19. 2 Corinthians 5:21, Isaiah 61:10, Romans 3:22, Isaiah 64:6 teach that the righteousness of man is as filthy rags but when we believe in Jesus Christ, His righteousness is imputed to us.

20. "H5291 - na`arah - Strong's Hebrew Lexicon (KJV)." No Pages. Cited 29 Mar 2019. https://www.blueletterbible.org//lang/lexicon/lexicon.cfm?Strongs=H5291&t=KJV.

21. "H1330 - bĕthuwlah - Strong's Hebrew Lexicon (KJV)." No Pages. Cited 29 Mar 2019. https://www.blueletterbible.org//lang/lexicon/lexicon.cfm?Strongs=H1330&t=KJV.

CHAPTER 3: WHO DO YOU WANT TO BE?

1. Hegai, These dictionary topics are from M.G. Easton M.A., D.D., Illustrated Bible Dictionary, Third Edition, published by Thomas Nelson, 1897. Public Domain, copy freely. https://www.biblestudytools.com/dictionary/hegai/

2. Notes on the Bible by Albert Barnes [1834]. Text Courtesy of Internet Sacred Texts Archive.

CHAPTER 4: THE IMPORTANCE OF RESPECT

1. Benson Commentary on the Old and New Testaments, Text Courtesy of BibleSupport.com. Used by Permission. Bible Hub

2. Benson Commentary on the Old and New Testaments, Text Courtesy of BibleSupport.com. Used by Permission. Bible Hub

3. Exposition of the Entire Bible by John Gill [1746-63]. Text Courtesy of Internet Sacred Texts Archive.

4. Jamieson, Fausset, and Brown in A Commentary, Critical, Experimental and Practical on the Old and New Testaments

5. You can read more about the rights and responsibilities of a Jamaican citizen at the National Library of Jamaica https://nlj.gov.jm/civics/.

You can read more about the rights and responsibilities of a citizen of the United States of America at the Official Website of the Department of Homeland Security, Citizenship Rights, and Responsibilities, https://www.uscis.gov/citizenship/learners/citizenship-rights-and-responsibilities.

If you are not a citizen of any of these two countries, a simple search on Google "rights of a citizen of [name of country]" should bring up the official rights of a citizen for your country.

CHAPTER 5: CREATING A CULTURE OF CARE

1. A similar practice is observed in Genesis 23:3-15. After Sarah died, Abraham went to the Hittite elders to purchase a piece of land to bury his wife. He wanted to buy a cave which belonged to

Ephron. But Ephron refused to sell after he politely informed Abraham the value of the land. Abraham persisted and the two parried before finally, the Ephron agreed to sell the land for 400 shekels. This polite interchange was a typical bargaining practice at the time. NLT Chronological Life Application Study Bible, Tyndale House Publishers, Inc. (November 2, 2012) page 46-47.

The practice of taarof, as it is called, continues today. Iranians refuse what they want to accept as a way of showing honor to the other person. The Persian art of etiquette, By Julihana Valle, 14 November 2016, http://www.bbc.com/travel/story/20161104-the-persian-art-of-etiquette

2. Decision Making In Ancient Persia: Drunk And Sober, June 7, 2017, http://historybuffed.com/interesting/decision-making-ancient-persia-drunk-sober/

3. What is the meaning of sackcloth and ashes? https://www.gotquestions.org/sackcloth-and-ashes.html

4. While at Mount Sinai, the Israelites were told that they should not marry the Canaanites because they would turn their hearts away from God and cause Him to be angry with them Deuteronomy 7:3-4.

5. "G2409 - hiereus - Strong's Greek Lexicon (KJV)." No Pages. Cited 15 Apr 2019. https://www.blueletterbible.org//lang/lexicon/lexicon.cfm?Strongs=g2409&t=kjv.

CHAPTER 6: OUR ACTIONS MATTER

1. During King Darius' reign, an edict was passed making it illegal for people in the kingdom to pray to any other god or human for

30 days except the king. The punishment was to be cast into the lions' den. You can read the full story in Daniel 6.

2. King Nebuchadnezzar commanded that everyone should bow before his golden statue. The person who did not would be thrown into a fiery furnace. You can read the full story in Daniel 3.

3. Wikipedia contributors, "Xerxes I," Wikipedia, The Free Encyclopedia, https://en.wikipedia.org/w/index.php?title=Xerxes _I&oldid=895650741 (accessed May 6, 2019).

CHAPTER 7: WHAT ABOUT OUR FRIENDS?

1. The advice in the book of Proverbs works in much the same way a modern proverb does. It outlines a principle and is not always meant to be taken literally.

2. Apps like BibleGateway, YouVersion, and YouTube allow us to listen to the Bible. You can also use apps like Olive Tree to create a library of Bibles and biblical resources.

3. This quote has been attributed to Winnie the Pooh.

4. 5 Traits of A Good Friend, https://www.hebrews12endurance.com/traits-of-a-good-friend.html

5. This quote has been attributed to Andrew Grant.

6. 14 Rules That Make a Princess's Life Less Than Easy, https://brightside.me/wonder-people/14-rules-that-make-a-princesss-life-less-than-easy-406760/

CHAPTER 8: DON'T BE RULED BY ANGER

1. "H2534 - chemah - Strong's Hebrew Lexicon (KJV)." No Pages. Cited 8 Apr 2019. https://www.blueletterbible.org//lang/lexicon/lexicon.cfm?Strongs=h2534&t=kjv.

2. Benson Commentary on the Old and New Testaments, Text Courtesy of BibleSupport.com. Used by Permission

3. Darius's Empire, https://www.johndclare.net/AncientHistory/Alexander9.htm

4. A fire plan is a written document that tells each person what they should do in the event of a fire. To take it a step further, every home should have a plan of action in the case of fire or whatever natural disaster occurs most often in the area where you live. Each member of the family should know what needs to be done.

Fire Emergency Evacuation Plan and the Fire Procedure, https://www.firesafe.org.uk/fire-emergency-evacuation-plan-or-fire-procedure/

5. 7 Ways Anger Is Ruining Your Health, by Debbie Strong. Last Updated: 5/29/2015 https://www.everydayhealth.com/news/ways-anger-ruining-your-health/

6. 14 Warning Signs That Unforgiveness Is Eating You Alive (And What to Do About It), by Cylon George July 4, 2018, https://www.spirituallivingforbusypeople.com/unforgiveness

7. Ellicott's Commentary for English Readers, Text Courtesy of BibleSupport.com. Used by Permission.

8. Genocide is any attempt or intent to destroy completely, or in part, any national, ethnical, racial or religious group.

Read more about genocide at Office of the Un-Special Adviser on the Prevention of Genocide (OSAPG), https://www.un.org/ar/preventgenocide/adviser/pdf/osapg_anal ysis_framework.pdf

CHAPTER 9: IS FEAR STRENGTH OR A WEAKNESS?

1. Jamieson, Fausset, and Brown in A Commentary, Critical, Experimental and Practical on the Old and New Testaments

2. Exposition of the Entire Bible by John Gill [1746-63]. Text Courtesy of Internet Sacred Texts Archive.

3. The Pulpit Commentary, Electronic Database. Copyright © 2001, 2003, 2005, 2006, 2010 by BibleSoft, Inc., Used by permission Bible Hub

4. Notes on the Bible by Albert Barnes [1834]. Text Courtesy of Internet Sacred Texts Archive.

CHAPTER 10: PREPARING FOR SPIRITUAL WARFARE

1. This is what the LORD says: "When seventy years are completed for Babylon, I will come to you and fulfill my good promise to bring you back to this place" (Jeremiah 29:10 NIV).

2. How to Engage In Spiritual Warfare, Caribbean Women of Faith, https://www.cbnfaithwomen.com/2019/03/14/how-to-engage-in-spiritual-warfare/

CHAPTER 11: MY RELATIONSHIP WITH GOD

1. Ellicott's Commentary for English Readers, Text Courtesy of BibleSupport.com. Used by Permission.

2. "H7812 - shachah - Strong's Hebrew Lexicon (KJV)." No Pages. Cited 23 May 2019. https://www.blueletterbible.org//lang/lexicon/lexicon.cfm?Strongs=h7812&t=kjv.

3. Jamieson, Fausset, and Brown in A Commentary, Critical, Experimental and Practical on the Old and New Testaments

4. The Pulpit Commentary, Electronic Database. Copyright © 2001, 2003, 2005, 2006, 2010 by BibleSoft, Inc., Used by permission Bible Hub

5. New World Encyclopedia contributors, "Babylonian Exile," New World Encyclopedia, https://www.newworldencyclopedia.org/p/index.php?title=Babylonian_Exile&oldid=1016425 (accessed May 23, 2019).

6. Babylonia https://www.history.com/topics/ancient-middle-east/babylonia Babylonia, History.com Editors, HISTORY Access Date April 16, 2019 Publisher A&E Television Networks Last Updated August 21, 2018, Original Published Date February 2, 2018

7. The Editors of Encyclopaedia Britannica, Babylonian Captivity, Encyclopædia Britannica, Publisher: Encyclopædia Britannica, Inc., Date Published: April 09, 2019, https://www.britannica.com/event/Babylonian-Captivity, Access Date: May 23, 2019

8. Months of the Jewish Year Navigating the 12 months of the Hebrew calendar by MJL

https://www.myjewishlearning.com/article/months-of-the-jewish-year/

9. When Was Judah's 70-Year Babylonian Captivity? by John P. Pratt, Reprinted from The Ensign 28, No. 10 (October 1998), pp. 64-65. ©1998 by Corporation of the President of The Church of Jesus Christ of Latter-day Saints. All rights Reserved. https://www.johnpratt.com/items/docs/captivity.html

10. This series of YouTube videos provide various methods of studying the Bible: https://bit.ly/Bible4Beginners

11.   2   Timothy   2:15 https://www.hebrews12endurance.com/2Timothy2-15.html

CHAPTER 12: THE RIGHT WAY TO FIGHT

1. Exodus 20:13 NKJV

2. If you want to learn more about the sacrificial system, check out this series of blog posts: Finding Grace in Leviticus, https://www.hebrews12endurance.com/finding-grace-in-leviticus-menu.html

3. This date is referenced because according to historical records, Xerxes reigned from 486-465 BC. Esther was taken to Xerxes in the seventh year of his reign (Esther 2:16) which would have been circa 479 BC.

About the Author

Aminata Coote is a Christian author and blogger. She is passionate about teaching others how to study the Bible. She is a wife, mother, author, and follower of Jesus Christ who encourages women to spend time with God and root their identities in Christ so they'll be able to focus on running the race God has set before them.

Official Author Website: https://aminatacoote.com/
Faith Website: https://www.hebrews12endurance.com/
Twitter handle: https://twitter.com/AminataCoote
Facebook: https://www.facebook.com/AminataCoote/
Instagram: https://www.instagram.com/AminataCoote/

Other Books by Aminata Coote
How To Find Your Gratitude Attitude
Face Your Fears: Choose Faith Over Fear
7 Lessons on Endurance from Hebrews 12:1-2
Through God's Eyes: Marriage Lessons for Women

Claim your free e-book!

Get a free copy of Aminata Coote's book **Face Your Fears** when you sign up for her Readers' Group. Enter URL https://bit.ly/2TttQ4K to get started:

More from Aminata Coote

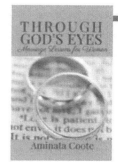

Marriage is hard work.

Those words have never been truer as the enemy does his best to destroy one of God's most sacred institutions. Learn what God has to say about marriage and claim the relationship He wants you to experience with your spouse.

Through God's Eyes: Marriage Lessons for Women

Let us run with endurance the race set before us.

This invitation in Hebrews 12 is one most Christians are familiar with. These seven lessons will encourage you to dust off your running shoes and chase after your Savior again.

7 Lessons on Endurance from Hebrews 12:1-2

What would you do if your fear didn't hold you back?

This 7-day challenge is an invitation to look at your fear and take steps to put it behind you. Wy walk in fear when you can choose faith instead?

Face Your Fear: Choose Faith Over Fear

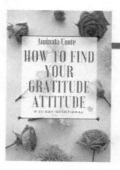

Gratitude is a choice—especially on those hard days when life feels difficult.

This 21-day devotional encourages you to dig deep to find the cause of your ingratitude until you can fully embrace your gratitude attitude.

How To Find Your Gratitude Attitude

For more information, check out her author page on Amazon.com https://bit.ly/CooteAMZ.

Made in the USA
Columbia, SC
25 September 2023

23372196R00135